THE WALLACE STEVENS CASE

24.95

The

WALLACE STEVENS CASE

Law and the Practice
of Poetry

Thomas C. Grey

Harvard University Press
Cambridge, Massachusetts
London, England   1991

This book is printed on acid-free paper, and its binding materials
have been chosen for strength and durability.

Library of Congress Cataloging-in-Publication Data

Grey, Thomas C.
   The Wallace Stevens case: law and the practice of poetry / Thomas C. Grey.
      p. cm.
   Includes bibliographical references and index.
   ISBN 0-674-94577-8
   1. Stevens, Wallace, 1879-1955—Criticism and interpretation. 2. Stevens, Wallace.
1879-1955—Knowledge—Law. 3. Law and literature—United States. I. Title.
PS3537.T4753Z654 1991
811'.52—dc20

90-47968
CIP

Page 149 constitutes an extension of the copyright page.

For Barbara

Acknowledgments

Like anyone who writes about Wallace Stevens, I owe special thanks to the superb group of critics his poetry has attracted over the years, of whom Harold Bloom and Helen Vendler are only the most remarkable of many. I have tried to give credit wherever I knew I had been helped by a commentator's insights, but this far understates my debt.

Stanford Law School, its faculty and students, its library, staff, and administration, supplied the basic intellectual and material environment to sustain me throughout this foray across disciplinary lines, and also gave helpful financial support through the Claire and Michael Brown Estate; thanks to Dean Paul Brest, and to many others at the law school. A decade or so back, the Stanford Faculty Interpretation Seminar started me thinking about connections between law and literature; thanks to its organizers, and all its participants. Then a year in the stimulating atmosphere of the Stanford Humanities Center helped me focus those thoughts; thanks to past and present directors Ian Watt and Bliss Carnochan, and to the staff and Fellows. Finally, in the late stages of work on this manuscript, the Stanford Biography Seminar lent me its collective resources for a fruitful session; thanks to all, and special thanks to Pamela Herr, who suggested the subtitle.

At Harvard University Press, I must thank Michael Aronson for his energetic supervision of the project, and Maria Ascher for her careful editing of the manuscript.

I am grateful to many other fellow workers and friends. Marian Holys did good work on the manuscript. Jay Fowler and Carolyn Karr provided valuable research assistance. Patricia Parker gave me essential encouragement to go forward on the basis of an early sketch of the project, as did Diane Middlebrook, who also supplied an important piece of advice. David Luban and Helen Vendler provided valuable suggestions after reading parts of the manuscript. Others read the whole manuscript at one stage or another, and responded with morale-boosts and constructive criticisms: Alison Anderson, Madeleine Kahn, Susan Mann, Frank Michelman, Richard Posner, Robert Rabin, Richard Rorty, Robert Weisberg, and Steven Winter. Lawrence Joseph and Margaret Jane Radin not only read the whole manuscript, and were unstinting in their help and advice, but also gave the constant and sustaining encouragement of fellow law professorial Stevensians.

Over many hours taken from work on her own book, Barbara Babcock touched nearly every line of this one with her ruthlessly loving editorial pencil. Beyond that, her person is in every word of it: an example, a comfort, a delight.

Contents

The world was everything that was the case?
Open the case. Lift out the fabulous
Necklace . . .

—James Merrill,
Mirabell: Books of Number, IX

But a politics
Of property is not an area
For triumphals. These are hymns appropriate to
The complexities of the world, when apprehended,
The intricacies of appearance, when perceived.

—Wallace Stevens,
"Reply to Papini"

Introduction

Not many years ago, I bemused some fellow law professors by allowing a student to receive law school credit for a poetry course. I would not have done that student a favor if I had gone on to recommend him to a law firm as "quite a poet." The profession generally assumes that nothing could be more remote from law's theory and practice than poetry. While accepting that assumption myself, I occasionally used to wonder whether the time I spent reading my favorite poet, the lawyer Wallace Stevens, was really time spent off the job. Then over the last two years, while writing about the place of American pragmatism in legal theory, I felt, again and more strongly, that my attraction to Stevens had something to do with my work as a law teacher and scholar. That led me on to this inquiry into what might connect Stevens's poetry with the concerns of the practicing or the academic bar.

A recent development in legal scholarship has lent some outside support to this unlikely enterprise. The proponents of the new law-and-literature movement now urge that lawyers, or at least legal theorists, can learn from literary texts. For example, in a 1986 article in the *Harvard Law Review,* the legal theorist Robin West used her readings of some of Franz Kafka's stories to attack the tendency of lawyers who take their theories from economics to equate the law's Reasonable Person with Economic Man. Some legal scholars found her project absurd. But the most important of the legal economists, Richard Posner, took the challenge seriously indeed; he both responded to Professor West's article, and went on to write a book-length critique of the whole emerging tendency to base legal arguments on literary works.

Judge Posner insisted that Kafka's training and daily work as a lawyer do not mean that his stories addressed legal issues, and supported his argument with a sentence that seemed to speak straight to me: "Wallace Stevens was also a lawyer . . . but no one supposes that Stevens's . . . poetry is about law."[1] Actually, with the current law-and-literature ferment, a few legal scholars and teachers now *do* suppose that Stevens's poetry is in some way "about law." Thus, in an article defending the law's specialized professional language, the dean of a major law school quotes extensively from Stevens, whom he describes as "not only a poet but also a lawyer."[2] Another respected legal scholar assigns several of Stevens's poems in a required introductory course in legal theory and method—and these two are not alone in acknowledging Wallace Stevens as a kind of lawgiver.[3]

With this kind of encouragement, I decided to try to articulate the intimations of connection I had felt between Stevens's poetry and my own thinking about law. I knew that Judge Posner was only stating the obvious when he denied any legal significance to the poetry of the lawyer Stevens. On the face of it, that body of difficult lyric-meditative verse has nothing at all to do with the legal world in which the poet made his living, and in which lawyers practice today. Stevens did not, as poets like Auden and Browning have, make law one of his subjects, nor did he, like Shakespeare or Donne, bring legal concepts or imagery to bear on other subjects.

Even if Stevens's poetry did echo his law work, most lawyers and legal scholars would still assign it only a decorative role in legal discourse—something to quote in an after-dinner speech, or to spice up an otherwise prosaic opinion. Thus, the profession finds strange indeed the far-reaching suggestions of the most prominent law-and-literature proponent, James Boyd White. He urges that lawyers should assimilate "the judicial opinion" to "the poem," and that, more generally, we should substitute a "poetic" for a "theoretical" form of writing and reading in legal education and practice.[4]

Professor White believes the study of literature can teach lawyers to reconceive their practice as a craft centrally organized around skills of humane writing and reading, rather than as the calculus of signals and sanctions portrayed by economic models of

2

the legal system. Other theorists, like Professor West, think literature can make lawyers and judges more empathic, more aware of the varieties of culture and the nuances of individual motivation, than can economics and rational-choice theory.[5] Still others, like Ronald Dworkin, stress the centrality of interpretation to both literary criticism and law, and argue that the study of literary hermeneutics can bring new insights to the lawyer's task of construing contracts and constitutions.[6]

To all these theories, Judge Posner has proposed an across-the-board countermanifesto on the side of professional common sense. He advocates a scholarly wall of separation that he intends as protection for both realms: "The literary should be a sphere apart" from the legal.[7]

In this book at least, I do not want to spend much time debating the place of literature in law, or even poetry in law, at the level of these abstract pronouncements pro and con. Yet without the movement of thought that the manifesto writers dramatize, I doubt that I would have pursued my own inchoate intimations into print. Moreover, an inquiry like this one is naturally seen as contributing a case study to the theoretical debate, and hence weighing for or against the admission of literary texts into the legal canon. So I should at least confess my conflicting initial impulses on the broad theories. These impulses form part of this study's "philosophy," in the lay meaning that William James gave to the word: one's "more or less dumb sense" of "the total push and pressure of the cosmos" as it bears on the issue at hand.[8]

On the side of separation, I feel the stylistic appeal of generic integrity; law is law, poetry is poetry, and efforts to splice or interanimate the two genres are likely to breed ungainly hybrids. Further, anyone who both knows legal academia and cares for poetry must pale a little at the thought of the law professoriate clumping through the garden in search of specimens to be displayed, dried and paraphrased, in law review footnotes. Finally, I think the idea that literature has direct and immediately practical uses for lawyers and judges has been seriously oversold. The rhetoric used for this oversell has then fed the academic tendency to

3

emphasize law's discourse at the expense of its actions and their material consequences. As a result, law-and-literature study in general (law-and-poetry study all the more) always risks falling into an apolitical and precious legal aestheticism.[9]

On the other side, the blurring or mixing of genres has its renovative attractions; there might be a *fisherman's* version of Wallace Stevens's observation that to a poet "moon-vines are moon-vines and tedious [but] moon-vines trained on fishing-twine are something else."[10] And as for the fragility of poetry, most of the time I doubt that there is any protected poetic garden for the lawyers to violate; the poets seem always to have been out of Eden, with the world all before them. A similar point bears on the central question of the practical and political consequences of studying law from a literary perspective; I cannot shake off the sense that we lawyers should be able to learn something useful from poets, those ultimate specialists in language, about our own inescapably linguistic business.

Thus, urges both to sharpen and to blur (or cross) the genre-boundary between law and poetry coexist for me, and this fact brings me to my third guiding impulse, one that is linked to my intuition that Stevens's poetry bears on law by way of the concerns of the American pragmatists. A pragmatist bias toward the importance of situation and context makes me suspicious of giving central focus to broad pronouncements on the Relation of Law to Literature (or Law to Poetry), whether assimilationist or separationist. My main interest is in what the poetry of Wallace Stevens has to do with law. I pursue that question largely animated by my own "dumb sense" of the conflicting impulses noted above—while recognizing, also in good pragmatist fashion, that even the most abstract theories can modify dumb sense when they give it voice and submit it to critical reflection.[11]

Thus, I undertake this study with impulses toward keeping law separate from poetry (common sense), toward exploring their connections (those intimations), and against overgeneralizing on the subject (pragmatism)—"of three minds, / Like a tree / In which there are three blackbirds."[12] Quoting these words of Stev-

4

ens's brings me to still another motive, the pull of his poetry itself. In pursuing my study, I hope to carry with me fellow unprofessional poetry readers, lawyers and others—even some who may in the past have been put off by this particular poet's provocative inaccessibility.

In my experience the poems eventually do yield up many of their secrets, while always keeping something back. Part of Stevens's lasting appeal is his capacity to evoke, in a wholly secular world, moments of wounding and healing mystery when "Intangible arrows quiver and stick in the skin / And I taste at the root of the tongue the unreal of what is real."[13]

Let me offer a sample, concededly law-unrelated. In what may have been his last poem, "Of Mere Being," Stevens wrote of a "gold-feathered bird" in "a palm at the end of the mind"; the bird sings a song "without human meaning . . . a foreign song," and so teaches "that it is not the reason / That makes us happy or unhappy." The poem ends thus:

> The bird sings. Its feathers shine.
> The palm stands on the edge of space.
> The wind moves slowly in the branches.
> The bird's fire-fangled feathers dangle down.[14]

If this hits home to you, you might also be tempted by some of the questions it raises for me. The last line, its gaudy diction standing out from the plain of its predecessors, suggests a bird on the verge of fiery death, with a hope of rebirth further off. Does this connect it to Shakespeare's vanished phoenix, the center of another mysterious poem?[15] The static verbs ("shine," "stands," "moves slowly," "dangle") seem to give an offsetting glossy print or freeze-frame quality to the scene's tropical luxuriance. How does this relate to the hint of flame to come? And I also wonder about the precise location of Stevens's palm tree ("at the end of the mind . . . on the edge of space"). Is it the boundary between the imagined and the real? And what does *that* mean here? Such questions, and more, leave me on edge myself, always ready to fall back into the poem again.

Still, as eager as I am for companionship in reading this poem and others, my main aim is neither to promote Stevens by introducing new readers to his poetry, nor to add some amateur explication to the splendid body of expert criticism already available. Rather, I intend first to show poetry-reading legal scholars and theorists that this poet can add to our understanding of law. Second, I reach out to literary scholars and those interested in interdisciplinary cultural studies, and to general readers as well, with the hope that my legal theorist's angle might admit a distinctive light on this poetry

My point for legal theorists, stated briefly, comes to something like this. We traditionally see legal disputes as posing binary choices: one side or the other wins; conduct is lawful or unlawful. The form of the judgment tends to induce in lawyers and legal theorists a matching binary approach to legal thought. Thus, we treat opposed legal principles and theories as if we must choose between them to maintain intellectual consistency, as if they were mutually contradictory mathematical theorems or scientific hypotheses. But plausible legal principles and theories are rarely precise enough to play such a role. They are better seen as guidelines, reminders of matters to be taken into account in judgment. They can thus readily coexist in useful tension, without contradiction, bringing to mind the opposed factors that the decision-maker should consider.

But legal thinkers resist this pragmatist middle way. Official jurisprudence favors the scientific or mathematical model, which has correct legal judgment following deductively from exact and impersonal principles. Given the usual binary character of legal thought, this official line then generates a jurisprudential opposition party that portrays legal judgments as entirely the result of individual intuition, creativity, or political will—this simply because those judgments are *not* dictated by the law's intellectual apparatus of principle, doctrine, and theory with the promised inexorability. Legal theory is too often characterized by absolutists and disappointed absolutists shouting past each other.

Wallace Stevens can speak to the lawyer or legal theorist as a

6

kind of therapist for the habitual and institutional rigidities of binary thought. Poetry is commonly seen in terms of an interactive opposition between romantic and classic: a dialectic, that is, between what Stevens called "imagination" and "reality," between creation and mimesis, between pride in the poet's power of invention and humility in the face of forces no power of invention can evade. The ability to hold conflicting generalizations in mind at the same time is one aspect of the special poets' virtue that Keats (speaking of Shakespeare) called "negative capability"—the ability to be "in uncertainties, mysteries, doubts, without any irritable reaching after fact and reason," capable of "remaining content with half-knowledge." [16]

In this century, Wallace Stevens has carried forward perhaps more than any other poet in English the Shakespearean and Keatsian tradition of negative capability. This makes him a unique spokesman for that philosophical middle way that in modern thought has come to be called pragmatism, a form of thought that in my view is especially suited to law and legal theory. Although poetry will never be *necessary* to legal education, the lawyer with access to Stevens and certain other poets has at hand a unique cultural resource—a reinforcement of the slender body of legal theory that emphasizes theoretical tolerance and flexibility as a significant professional virtue.

What can looking at Stevens in this way do for those of his readers and students who are not professionally concerned with the law? My hope is to at least test the bounds of the ivory tower in which Stevens's unfriendly critics, in collaboration with some admirers, confine him. When compared to the work of modern poets such as Yeats and Auden, Neruda and Milosz, Rich and Lorde, Stevens's poetry quite naturally seems hermetic. Yet to the extent it speaks to central issues of legal theory, it is not irrelevant to social and political concerns.

My argument divides roughly into two parts. In the first three chapters, I bring out the stark gap between Stevens's poetry and the usual concerns of lawyers; in the last three, I try to show how, despite that divide, the poetry nevertheless helps to articulate a pragmatist vision that contributes distinctively to legal theory. Chapter I considers Stevens's involvement with law in his own life. He was trained as a lawyer but worked for an insurance company. Did he do so as a lawyer or a businessman? I will examine why this question has mattered to some of his literary commentators, and conclude that any connection between his poetry and law does not turn on how he made his living. Stevens did indeed literally practice law, at least in a way, but the real question is whether his poetry should bring us to treat him as a lawyer in some more metaphorical sense—a "law-related" writer, a legal authority, an acknowledged legislator.

I then proceed to examine two approaches used by law-and-literature proponents to bring literary works into the legal canon, and I conclude that Stevens's poetry fails on both counts. From the unpeopled world of his verse he does not, so I argue in Chapter II, teach otherwise hard-hearted lawyers or judges the equitable virtue of fellow-feeling, in the way imaginative writers are often especially good at doing. Nor does he in his own life or writing promote Professor White's conception of law as an enterprise that is literary and even poetic because centrally involved with the untranslatable, nonpropositional aspects of language. Rather, as I show in Chapter III, Stevens sharply distinguished between a prosaically utilitarian, masculine, and coercive world of law on the one hand, and a shadowed imaginary, ambiguous, and androgynous world of poetry on the other.

Having rejected various likely connections between Stevens's poetry and law, in Chapter IV I turn to consider the other side. Stevens's poem "The Motive for Metaphor," which I examine in some detail, seems at first to confirm his belief in a separation between a poet's imagined land of metaphor and a harsh real world of power and literal speech. But a further look, both at the poem's words and at their context in the poet's life and times, suggests a breach in that wall in the capacity of language and imagination to contribute through metaphor to the construction of reality itself—an idea central to Stevens's poetry. In Chapter V, I widen the perspective by considering more generally whether

Stevens writes as a philosopher, and implicitly a legal philosopher, when he addresses his central poetic theme of the relation between imagination and reality by way of language. I conclude that his poetry on this theme embodies a philosophical (and specifically pragmatist) portrayal and account of the mind's workings—one that can be of special interest to the theoretically inclined lawyer. In Chapter VI, I further suggest how Stevens's poetic version of pragmatism bears on the debate between legal theorists who stress the (classical) rule of strict law and those who stress the (romantic) virtues of equitable discretion. I close by reformulating some important limits on my claims, and by arguing that there is a paradoxical affinity between pragmatism, with its mundane stress on the centrality of practice, and the expression of its theories in the form of poetry.

The balanced structure I have sketched here may suggest a balanced contribution to the law-and-literature debate: three chapters for separation, three for assimilation, bracketed by an introduction and conclusion judiciously giving fair weight to both sides. While not inaccurate, this description seems to me to miss the improbable character of the inquiry itself. My hypothesis is not the plausible claim that studying, say, *Billy Budd* or *The Trial* can contribute to our understanding of law; what I am talking about is the legal implications of *the poetry of Wallace Stevens*. It was with a sense that I had been sent on a most far-fetched and unpredictable venture that I set out to pursue my intimations of connection between Stevens's poetry and legal theory. I hope to have preserved some of that feeling in the following report on what I found in my explorations.

I

An Occupation, an Exercise, a Work

Perplexed, and longing to be comforted,
My question eagerly I did renew,
"How is it that you live, and what is it you do?"

—William Wordsworth
"Resolution and Independence"

An air of mystery hangs over Stevens's working life for most of his readers; we are curious about just what he did at the office, and about its relation to his poetry.[1] The curiosity is not idle or random, but stems from a sense that an inexplicable abyss divides the Stevens who made so respectable a bourgeois living as a vice-president of the Hartford Accident and Indemnity Company from the Stevens who wrote the gaudy, exotic, mysterious poetry for which he is remembered.

Some Stevens readers take positive delight at the idea of a virtuoso of separate lives, a disguise-artist of changing identities. For most, though, especially those most under the spell of the Romantic tradition, the division between Stevens's two lives bespeaks a self-alienation inconsistent with the prophetic and revelatory role that we expect the poet to play. The duplicity leaves us perplexed, even "longing to be comforted."

One way to consider the issue of disjunction in Stevens's life is to examine his job with an eye on the insignificant question of how it should be described. Intriguingly, commentators on Stevens's poetry turn out to divide into two groups, assigning him job titles in a way that roughly matches their evaluation of the poet's stature. Those who call Stevens a businessman, corporate executive, or insurance man tend to stress the incongruity between his art and his office work, and are more likely to make the criticism that his poetry is marginal, ivory-tower, and escapist. Conversely, those who call him a lawyer tend to see his work as relatively compatible with his writing, and generally regard him as a major poet speaking to central human concerns. Why the difference?

Before venturing an answer, let me note some basic facts about Stevens's life that are common ground between those who characterize him respectively as businessman and lawyer.[2] Born in Reading, Pennsylvania, on October 2, 1879, the son of a successful lawyer father and a housewife mother, Stevens had a childhood apparently happy, and unusual only in its few hints of his literary precocity. After three years at Harvard, where he spent much of his time writing conventional *fin-de-siècle* verse and editing the literary magazine, he went to New York City in 1900 to become a writer. After an unsuccessful year at journalism, he accepted his father's firm advice and followed his two brothers to law school. Three years later he joined the New York Bar. But he could not make a living in private practice, and in 1908 he took a job with an insurance company handling claims made on its surety bonds.

In 1916, he moved to Connecticut to take care of surety-bond claims for the Hartford Accident and Indemnity Company, a new subsidiary of a long-established fire insurance company. The Hartford put Stevens in charge of its fidelity and surety-claims division in 1918,[3] and he ran it until 1955, past the company's compulsory retirement age and up to a few weeks before his death from cancer at the age of seventy-five.[4] He was promoted to vice-president in 1934, but declined all opportunities for further corporate advancement,[5] while so mastering his small and specialized domain that he was considered "the dean of surety-claims men in the whole country,"[6] and "absolutely the diamond in the tiara" of his company.[7] The money he made at his work largely freed him from the financial worries common to most poets.

Agreement on these facts, many of them available for years, has not dispelled the sense of strangeness Stevens's readers have felt about his work at the Hartford. When he was alive, Stevens disliked the mystery, but, disliking personal publicity even more, he withheld disclosures that might have satisfied the persisting and annoying curiosity about the supposed incongruity between his poetry and how he made his living.[8] At the same time, he himself blurred the description of his work; in his letters, he three times called himself a lawyer, but once added, "I am in the insurance business."[9] Near the end of his life, in a speech, he equivocally alluded to his workplace as "a law office or a place of business."[10] Because he was by official title the vice-president of an insurance company, his obituary notices identified him as an executive, barely mentioning that he was a law graduate.[11]

The question of Stevens's occupational identification has, as I noted, been connected to the evaluation of his poetry, with "business" partisans tending to the less favorable judgments. John Berryman's wry elegy "So Long? Stevens" illustrates the point. Conceding that Stevens's art ("Mutter we all must as well as we can. / He mutter spiffy") was "flourishing," "brilliant," perhaps even "ever-fresh," Berryman nevertheless found something "missing . . . at the man's heart"; the poetry's "metaphysics" smothered its "physics," and threatened to render it finally "monotonous."[12] Thus, with a few words Berryman summons the litany of complaints against Stevens as poet. He is (to use a phrase of Marianne Moore's) "the meditative man with the perfunctory heart":[13] maker of clever but ultimately unsatisfying word-magic, narrowly verbal, hermetic; early, an effete and frivolous dandy; later, fleshless, dryly intellectual; always removed from the central life-world of society, ordinary people, and normal emotions.[14]

Berryman's poem establishes its tone of critique in opening lines that emphasize the incongruity between Stevens's poetry and his working life:

> He lifted up, among the actuaries,
> a grandee crow. Ah ha & he crowed good.
> That funny money-man.

Just as Christ, in ironic fulfillment of Isaiah's prophecy, was lifted up between thieves, so Stevens "lifted up" among actuaries; his strange work was with insurance and money (even, in a pun, "funny money"). There is no mention of law.[15]

12

These lines are so effective because an insurance company vice-presidency, a grandeeship among the actuaries, seems an unsuitable job for a poet. Poetry is supposed to have its being "where executives / Would never want to tamper."[16] The corporate executive is a capitalist, and the capitalist as poet is an oxymoron, an unassimilable monstrosity. Mary McCarthy exploits the same stereotype to achieve the same effect when she describes a fictional poet, probably modeled on Stevens, as "John D. Rockefeller drenched in attar of roses."[17] Capitalists may collect but not produce art. If by any chance they do produce it, they are expected to do so, consumerlike, as dilettantes: thus, to stress the business side of Stevens's work feeds into the standard unflattering portrayal of him as an isolated sensualist, a gourmet of the spirit as well as the body, a finicky connoisseur of fine foods and wines, rare pictures and books, and exotic images, finding his *materia poetica* in bric-a-brac.[18]

Frank Lentricchia is only the latest commentator to paint Stevens as an unhappy hedonist and a compulsive never-satisfied consumer, and hence, in Lentricchia's strongly political criticism, an archetypal representative of the alienation and decadence of late capitalism. Not surprisingly, he characterizes the poet occupationally as one who rose "to the corporate top of his business world."[19] Conversely, many Stevens admirers who perceive him as a businessman feel dissonance. Thus, a young commentator, Bernard Heringman, noted that "the whole idea of his being such a businessman and so devoted to his insurance work bothered me a little."[20] Likewise, admirers attending a Stevens reading were disappointed, so John Malcolm Brinnin reported, because they "had come to see Wallace Stevens the romantic poet and found themselves looking at a business executive."[21]

When Peter Brazeau's oral biography of Stevens appeared in 1983, with its rich detail on the poet's office work, it lent support to his admirers' efforts to reduce the sense of dissonance between Stevens's poetry and the rest of his life. Reviewing the book, Frank Doggett and Dorothy Emerson wrote that it would serve finally to "correct those who refer to Stevens as an insurance writer or salesman. Everyone should now know that he was a lawyer specializing in the law of bonding, mostly with surety claims."[22] The relief is evident; a career in law meant that Stevens's workaday and poetic worlds were not, after all, so incongruous.

The claim of incongruity had long been a target for Stevens's champions. In 1960, Frank Kermode, one of the first British critics to place Stevens in the top rank of modern poets, protested that "attention of the wrong kind" was being given to the poet's "double life," supposedly divided between art and an unsuitable kind of work. As one concerned to minimize the duplicity of that life, Kermode described Stevens not as an executive but as an "insurance lawyer."[23] Similarly and more recently, Milton Bates, in his fine critical biography, has attacked the "facile dichotomy . . . between the businessman and the poet."[24] Bates went on to emphasize Stevens's work as a lawyer, noting the legal terms used in his poems, and speculating ingeniously that his lawyer's experience with legal fictions might have contributed to his central poetic concept of a "supreme fiction."[25]

It is quite natural that admirers of his poetry should prefer to think of Stevens as a lawyer; to see the reasons for this preference is to see part of the subliminal appeal of the law-and-literature movement. The lawyer is a much older social type than the capitalist, and as a type can still be squeezed, alongside the poets, into the category of those scribes through whom the human race "writes down / The eccentric propositions of its fate."[26] Even though the poetic hearse-horse often snickers when the lawyer goes by, a number of effective cultural archetypes (mostly pre-Romantic and preindustrial) connect law to letters in the imagery and rhetoric of humanistic tradition.

Thus, Hesiod, at the dawn of Western poetry, wrote that a king, conceived mainly as a judge, a man of law, needs the assistance of the Muses to endow him with the "smooth and unerring speech" that can gain him popular honor and bring "to great disagreements a skillful solution."[27] And David, warrior and "sweet psalmist," had the word of the Lord in his tongue that he might speak justly as king-judge of Israel.[28] Examples can be multi-

14

plied: the classical rhetoricians taught the techniques of eloquence to both poets and lawyers; the Icelandic sagas portray warrior heroes who combine poetic and legal prowess; the ideal of Ciceronian republican eloquence linked law and letters in the early American republic;[29] in poetry's most famous manifesto, Shelley declared poets to be, if not themselves lawyers, at least "legislators";[30] and Matthew Arnold preached that poetry's "sweetness and light," by promoting an ideal of "the best self," could help channel the anarchic spirit of revolution into the "due course of law."[31]

Such slogans and archetypes make it plausible for Professor White to ask, "Is the Judge Really a Poet?" (in a chapter with an epigraph taken from Stevens), and then to answer in the affirmative.[32] Resonant images like these have also comforted those struggling with their own or others' doubts about the integrity or centrality of their own work, as well as of Stevens's poetic achievement. "Poet-lawyer" promises to help overcome unhappy stereotypes of soullessly philistine lawyers and socially marginal humanists. "Poet–insurance executive" merely sounds awkwardly incongruous.

What, then, does the evidence show on the question of Stevens's occupation? Brazeau's book supplies a good deal of information about what the poet did at work. Stevens was by title a corporate executive, named in 1934 to be one of only four vice-presidents of an important American insurance company. But the reminiscences collected from fellow workers make clear that he "was not in any way a typical corporate executive."[33] He spent little time managing the work of subordinates, and ostentatiously avoided advising or deliberating with his fellow officers on company policy. Both before and after his promotion, he kept his small department to himself, a "prince in his principality," and ran it by doing its most important work personally, while delegating the rest with virtually no supervision.[34] He hired and fired his subordinates, but they were few and there was little turnover, so this could not have taken much of his time.[35]

On a typical working day, Stevens came to his office around

nine, read his mail, then turned to the stack of files of claims requiring review, and worked on them systematically through the day.[36] He was renowned both for his steady diligence at work ("the grindingest guy . . . in executive row") and for his meticulous attention to detail; he left a clear desk at the end of each day, and did not take work home.[37] Stevens stayed in his office, cherishing his solitude as he ground through his files. A number of colleagues recall him reacting with annoyance when interrupted, even for a business purpose, or continuing to work, head down, for long minutes as they silently waited.[38] No office politician, he was often famously undiplomatic, with superiors as well as subordinates, peers, outside agents, and other sources of company business.[39] And as Stevens himself once wrote, his kind of work was so exclusively a matter of files and papers that he found it hard "to distinguish himself from the papers" and came "almost to believe that he and papers constitute a single creature."[40]

What Stevens was doing as he pored over those files was deciding the disposition of the larger claims made on surety bonds issued by his company. A surety bond is a promise by the insurer to pay a legal obligation of an insured; its purpose is to assure third parties who are at risk of loss if the insured becomes insolvent. To take the most common example, a builder might have to post a performance surety bond in order to get a construction job; the bond means that if the builder doesn't finish the job or botches it, the insurance company as surety will pay the resulting damages to the other party, even if the builder has gone broke in the meantime.[41]

As Stevens reviewed surety claims, he was making both legal and business judgments. On the legal side, he had to decide whether the claim was valid. Did the insured builder, for example, breach its contract? The insurance company could assert any defense available to the builder (for example, breach of a condition on the part of the claimant); deciding whether such a defense existed required close investigation of the facts and review of the original contract. On this ground, the "narrow" and "arcane" field of suretyship law, Stevens was widely respected for his expertise.[42] He was also renowned for calling the claims in an almost judicial manner. He was "very fair" to the point of "mercy," sometimes not asserting technical defenses; on the other hand, when he was sure the claim was bad, he was "tough as nails," and resistant to appeals from within the company based on corporate image or customer good will.[43]

If Stevens rejected a claim and the company was sued, he would hire a local lawyer to defend the case in the place where it would be tried. Stevens would instruct the outside lawyer through a letter reviewing the facts of the case and setting out the company's substantive legal position; he would then step out of the case, delegating all decisions on procedure and litigation strategy.[44] Only occasionally would he reenter a farmed-out case, typically to approve or help negotiate a settlement. In this capacity, he was decisive but sometimes too brusque, once so insulting an opposing lawyer that Stevens had to leave before negotiations could continue. As his Hartford colleague Manning Heard recalls: "Mr. Stevens was on a diet and he wasn't in too good a humor anyway—he called [government counsel] a silly old fool . . . Mr. Stevens was not a good bargainer. He was too impatient. He . . . didn't relish a skirmish with a mentality that he considered a little lower than his."[45] Still, they settled the more-than-million-dollar claim for a half-million.

Although Stevens stayed clear of corporate policy, an important aspect of his work involved pure business judgment. When he judged a claim to be valid, there remained, in contractor bond cases, the decision whether to pay off the bond or attempt to finish the work contracted for. Here is where Stevens achieved his greatest reputation; he was "a very imaginative claims man." The industry's rule of thumb was, "If you had a contractor that defaulted, don't try to finish the contract; you'll lose your pants." But Stevens frequently "violated that principle, and he finished contracts, and he was always pretty successful."[46] The decision required evaluating which contracts could still be performed for less than the damages payable to the other party, and thus at a profit to the company. Good judgment on such matters required

17

being "highly practical, realistic," qualities at the furthest remove from the "fantasy" of "poetry and all that's involved in poetry." Or so said one colleague—another stressed Stevens's "psychic intuitiveness" about these cases.[47] It was in connection with this ability of Stevens's that colleagues came to judge him "the dean of surety claims men in the whole country," the one of whom peers at other companies invariably said, "Oh, hell, he must be right."[48]

Though Stevens had and used legal training and skills in his job, he did not, in the full sense in which the profession uses the phrase, "practice law." He neither appeared in court nor advised clients, and so did not have to be, and at least for many years was not, a member of the bar.[49] His company was not a client; until 1934 he was its employee, and thereafter one of its officers. Nor did those close to him think of him as a legal practitioner. "I don't think he'd have been a practicing lawyer," said a lawyer-colleague; he would have been "unsuccessful" as a "practicing lawyer," added another. "He . . . didn't want to practice law," said Manning Heard, adding (in a distinction whose metaphysics may be difficult to outsiders) that though not a "practicing" lawyer, Stevens was certainly a "good" lawyer.[50]

So, finally, how did Wallace Stevens live, and what did he do? Little turns on whether we label Stevens's work law or business. He did not fit either stereotype. He was not a bar member; rather, he was a functionary in a large corporate bureaucracy, someone who neither went to court nor advised clients, and whose most valued skill was his business judgment. On the other hand, much of his work involved legal research and legal judgment; it was solitary, bookish, certainly not the typical work of a corporate executive.

Say, then, that he was an in-house lawyer who worked for an insurance company. This unromantic judgment cannot plausibly summon up the inspiring legal-literary archetypes of Hesiodic or biblical kings, bardic Icelandic advocates, Ciceronian republican statesmen, Shelleyan legislators, or Arnoldian priests of culture. Whether as business executive or lawyer, at work Stevens was a technician, a specialist. Calling his specialty "law" cannot bring with it the comfort his friendly critics long for on the issue of the integrity of his art with his working life—but calling it "business" should not perplex them, as it seems to do. Stevens really was, as his friend and colleague Wilson Taylor said, a "lawyer-businessman."[51] So, in Stevens's day, were many lawyers, and so, in our day of cost-effective and profit-maximizing law firm management, are most.

The interest in the designation of Stevens's occupation rests on a distinction, implicit in some of the manifestos for the law-and-literature movement but at best obsolescent as a matter of social reality, between inevitably philistine businessmen and more refined, hence potentially humanist, participants in the learned professions. But if a man in an expensive gray suit who works in an office cannot find material for poetry in such a life, that fact disqualifies modern lawyers as much as businessmen. Of course, there is life outside work, too, on which the flanneled bourgeois may draw. But are production, trade, and finance really intrinsically unpoetic subjects?

Mammon may have been the "least erected spirit that fell / From Heav'n," yet Milton gave him great lines protesting risky military adventures, and praising the prosperous pursuit of something like strip-mining and real-estate development under the protection of sound conservative government.[52] "Whatever interests the rest interests me," wrote Walt Whitman, and he included "banks, tariffs, steamships, factories, stocks, stores, real estate and personal estate." Marianne Moore said the poet should not "discriminate against 'business documents and / school books'; all these phenomena are important."[53] Philip Larkin, in one of his poems, described the selling routine of a 1920s farm supply merchant to a provincial hotel, and in another captured in four words the "uncaring / Intricate rented world" of the generic business office.[54] Stevens himself believed that "the whole world is material for poetry," and specifically that "money is a kind of poetry."[55] In a library copy of *Opus Posthumous,* I once found next to that last adage an obscenity scrawled by a reader who hated him for saying it. Smiters of the philistines are often smitten by foolishness themselves, complacent lawyers and resentful literati in their different ways.

In Stevens's case, though, there is a further ironic disjunction, which helps maintain his readers' persisting sense that the poet's daily walks between home and office were mysterious crossings. This sober citizen, this successful and conservative lawyer–insurance executive, so well situated to write the poetry of money, of real and personal estate, had in fact no vocation for it. The toad, work, had no place in his imaginary garden; the poems mostly (and most successfully) address the permanent lyric subjects— lamentation at loss and death, and praise to the occasional epiphanic mating of sense with imagination. He wished to sing "the heroic effort to live expressed / as victory," and could not do so with regard to law and commerce: "a politics / Of property is not an area / For triumphals."[56] No more "at home in / Our interpreted world" than his great contemporary, the ecstatic solitary Rilke, Stevens found the spur for his art in the pain of an alienation from those aspects of his own world that he called "normal" and "central":

> From this the poem springs: that we live in a place
> That is not our own and, much more, not ourselves
> And hard it is in spite of blazoned days.[57]

No one was better at portraying just how hard, and how bare, it was:

> He is not here, the old sun,
> As absent as if we were asleep.
>
> The field is frozen. The leaves are dry.
> Bad is final in this light.[58]

Out of the dark barren cold arose compensating triumphals, but the pleasures they celebrated were not such as are usually thought to drive society's great machine:

Bare night is best. Bare earth is best. Bare, bare,
Except for our own houses, huddled low
Beneath the arches and their spangled air,
Beneath the rhapsodies of fire and fire,
Where the voice that is in us makes a true response,
Where the voice that is great within us rises up,
As we stand gazing at the rounded moon.[59]

When a lawyer-executive in an "immaculate pearl-gray suit, looking very smooth and pink above it,"[60] speaks thus, he creates an incongruity too intriguing to wish or explain away. At the same time, he tends to baffle the quest of a lawyer in search of professional instruction.

II

The Unpeopled World

Life is an affair of people not of places. But for me life is an
affair of places and that is the trouble.

—Wallace Stevens, "Adagia"

What call'st thou solitude? . . .
. . . . .
. . . Thy Realm is large.

—John Milton, *Paradise Lost,* VIII

My central question is whether the poetry of Wallace Stevens, a
lawyer more or less, was more, or less, law related. To address
that question, I turn, in the next two chapters, from the census
taker's job of occupational classification to a kind of law professor's
doctrinal discussion, and in the last three to a lawyer's version of
literary commentary.

The doctrine to be elucidated and applied is that of the
law-and-literature movement. As a summary of its teaching, I
propose a continuum, at the poles of which are two kinds of
justification for accepting literary works into the legal canon:
psychological and linguistic. Psychologically oriented law-and-
literature theorists argue that literature can help lawyers and law-
makers understand and empathize with people and human conflicts in ways that more scientific sources of knowledge cannot.
Linguistically oriented theorists say that law should be understood as a discursive, rhetorical, ideological practice, rather than
as a set of signals or clear commands backed by sanctions; and
that this form of practice is understood better by analogy to the
way language is used in literature than to the way it is used in
science or analytic philosophy.

The two approaches are not mutually inconsistent, and some writers, like James Boyd White, give them equal force, proposing law as both morally humanitarian and culturally humanistic.[1] Others, like Robin West and the late Robert Cover, suspect that the linguistic approach diverts too much attention from the violent and coercive aspects of law; these theorists stress the psychological use of literary materials as sources of empathy and community, commonly with special stress on law's need for insight into the perspectives of those traditionally excluded from power.[2] Conversely, linguistically oriented law-and-literature proponents might embrace literature as well suited to teach lawyers both the constitutive character and the instability and indeterminacy of discursive practices, while eschewing the psychological-humanist themes of the universal human heart, the unique individual, and the especially empathic insights or communitarian tendencies of the literary imagination.[3]

At first it seems that justifications for including Stevens's poetry within the legal canon must lie toward the linguistic rather than the psychological or empathic pole of the continuum. From very early on in his life, Stevens felt, and regretted, a lack of warmth and human sympathy in himself. As a college student, boarding with a family that had fallen on hard times, he wrote in his journal that while over the course of a month he had "never noticed the pathos of their condition," one day's visit had brought tears to a friend's eyes. "I am too cold for that," he sadly concluded. The problem was not any lack of passion, but that his emotions flowed toward places, objects, and art, not people. The entry follows by five days one in which he had written: "It is quite impossible for me to express any of the beauty I feel to half the degree that I feel it."[4]

A half-century later, Stevens's company chauffeur, Naaman Corn, who often drove him on weekend shopping orgies and who observed his sometimes lordly ways with his family and others, put the point pungently: having chauffeured the boss to receive an honorary Doctorate of Humane Letters, Corn, focusing on the word "humane," thought the honor should go to someone who "had done something for humanity" and so, "my goodness alive, look like they could [have] picked on somebody else."[5] And two years before his death Stevens wrote, as if from an old hunger, "I nourish myself on books, nature, this and that, music—so rarely on the good friendships of men and women."[6]

Stevens's poetry came from his life, and throughout that life he inhabited an "unpeopled" world of vividly experienced places and objects: a world of reading, writing, and long solitary walks. ("He disposes the world in categories, thus: / The peopled and the unpeopled. In both, he is / Alone.")[7] Isolated and relatively apolitical, he took for his subjects poetry itself and his own thought processes, and for his imagery the phenomena of nature. Though he was a passionate poet, and not the decorative miniaturist or dry epistemologist some would make him, the passions most directly expressed in his poems were those at furthest remove from the normal purview of the legal system.

Stevens's own wistful words at the head of this chapter supply a text for commentary on his personal isolation. While he was growing up in Reading, he "always walked a great deal, mostly alone, and mostly on the hill, rambling along the side of a mountain." Later he discovered books, and "used to stay up all hours . . . [reading] Poe and Hawthorne."[8] He fit well into a home dominated by his father, "one of the most uncommunicative of men"; it was "rather a curious place, with all of us in different parts of it, reading."[9]

Half a century later, when his niece visited him in Connecticut, she found the same basic pattern: "The family didn't congregate: at the table for dinner, and then afterward up to their cells."[10] The family consisted of Wallace Stevens; his wife, Elsie Moll Stevens, whom he married in 1909 and who would survive him; and their only child, Holly, born in 1924, who left home in the early 1940s. The Stevens marriage was stoically maintained, in the manner of their class and time, in the face of nearly total incompatibility. They had few guests to the house. This was at least in part because Elsie Stevens, in the grip of a deep "persecution complex," was likely to cause scenes; some have suggested that Wallace Stevens may have taken the initiative in isolating her, and then used her neurosis (which was perhaps partly a result of her isolation) as an excuse to protect his own solitude.[11]

Nor was Stevens deeply engaged in personal relations outside his marriage. During Holly's childhood, he was the typical absentee father of his time.[12] He had broken with his own father over his marriage (Elsie's family was socially suspect), his parents had died without the breach's being repaired, and for decades thereafter Stevens had little contact with his Reading family. I have already described the brusquely solitary demeanor he maintained at his office. His life in Hartford prevented any extensive personal contact with fellow poets, writers, or artists. He did form friendships through his poetry, but carried these on mainly through letters—another kind of writing at which he excelled.[13]

While Stevens led an unusually solitary life, he did have some close friends, including, for many years, Judge Arthur Powell, an Atlanta lawyer whom he met in the early 1920s. Still, since they were together at most for a few weeks a year, this too was mostly a friendship by mail.[14] Closer to home, Stevens made a few personal friends in his working world; one colleague called him "a man who had close friends or no friends."[15] Late in life, renewing long-severed family ties, he established a relationship with two nieces who were very fond of "Uncle Wallace."[16] And he and his daughter became close after she was grown.[17]

Other reports further soften the well-attested picture of the isolated and imposing patriarch. Stevens could be generous to subordinates, as in the case of Richard Sunbury, a young man he guided to and through law school.[18] He gave unstinting and uncomplaining financial support to his brother Garrett during hard times.[19] Often anonymously, he donated money to fellow writers and struggling poetry journals.[20] In short, Stevens could be both a charming and a generous man when he focused his attention on other people. The fact remains, though, that he rarely did.

Stevens established his adult pattern of office work, reading, writing, and long solitary walks while he was a single law student and lawyer in New York. After some variation during his early married years there and in Hartford, the years that produced his first major poetry, the pattern was more substantially disrupted after the birth of his daughter in 1924, and for the next six years Stevens wrote almost nothing.[21] After 1930, settling into a routine bounded by office tasks and the rituals of an unhappy marriage, he reestablished his old habits of work, reading, writing, and walks, which he maintained rigorously until near his death in 1955. Of those years, not one passed, Harold Bloom judges, without "the writing of a great poem"—a record of "persistence and diversity of strength" that Bloom calls "a glory almost unique in the poetry of the last several centuries."[22]

These glorious poems are, as the poet's life suggests they would be, much more about places than about people. True, personae flock through them, but whether fictional, historical, or taken from Stevens's acquaintanceship, they do not emerge as living characters. When a poem ends, "Goodbye, Mrs. Pappadopoulos, and thanks," we have really never met the lady; indeed, that is one of the points of the poem.[23] She is a prop, and other characters in other poems are likewise props, or aspects of the poet himself, or archetypes such as the father or mother, the interior paramour, the spectre of the spheres, the necessary angel. The poems neither tell stories nor portray individuals distinct from the poet.

The unpeopled character of Stevens's poetry is not unusual for lyric or meditative verse, which often takes as its subject the relation of one character, the poet, to one setting, the natural world. Stevens fits the pattern: his only narrative is the fragmentary and usually implicit partial autobiography of his own poetic development;[24] his only drama, the struggle of a creative imagination to find a home in a sometimes overwhelming, sometimes sustaining, but always alien environment.

In general, poetry of the kind Stevens wrote has played a minor role in the law-and-literature movement. Narrative has been the favored literary form for teaching lawyers the lessons stressed by the psychological approach: that human beings in their complexity depart from the script laid down for *homo economicus;* and that in life human beings can and do make "interpersonal comparisons of utility," whatever economists may say against the possibility of such a conjuring trick.[25] The narrative recounting of human action in problematic situations induces the reader to identify with varied characters and to assess ambiguous actions, and thereby to extend sympathies and refine moral sensibilities in a way that improves legal judgment: travel is broadening, practice makes perfect.[26] The typical Stevensian meditative "poem of the act of the mind"[27] represents an action as well, the writer's own action in forming a judgment and expressing it in words. But the question of the relevance of this kind of action-representation to the lawyer must await the next chapter, which considers the language-based approaches to law and literature.

Though other people are largely absent from Stevens's poems, passion is not; it is his longing for the absent other that gives the poems much of their power. As Helen Vendler has shown so well, they are not the merely decorative or cerebral exercises in verbal facility that his unsympathetic critics find them to be; the mind that created was not separate from the man who suffered.[28] When Stevens writes, as he so often does in one form or another, of the "dumbfoundering abyss / Between us and the object," his true subject is always something more emotionally compelling than epistemology; it is often the longing of a lonely man for his dead parents, or for a woman's love.[29] Stevens sometimes makes explicit his usually tacit substitution of "I-it" or human-to-nature relations for "I-thou" or human-to-human ones. Consider "Arrival at the Waldorf":

> Where the wild poem is a substitute
> For the woman one loves or ought to love
> One wild rhapsody a fake for another
>
> . . . . .
> After that alien, point-blank, green and actual Guatemala.[30]

27

Or "World without Peculiarity":

> The day is great and strong—
> But his father was strong, that lies now
> In the poverty of dirt.
>
> . . . . .
>
> What good is it that the earth is justified,
> That it is complete, that it is an end,
> That in itself it is enough?[31]

Or "The Auroras of Autumn":

> Farewell to an idea . . . The mother's face,
> The purpose of the poem, fills the room.
>
> . . . . .
>
> A wind will spread its windy grandeurs round
> And knock like a rifle-butt against the door.
> The wind will command them with invincible sound.[32]

Or the great love song to the earth that concludes "Notes toward a Supreme Fiction":

> Fat girl, terrestrial, my summer, my night
>
> . . . . .
>
> We shall return at twilight from the lecture
> Pleased that the irrational is rational,
> Until flicked by feeling, in a gildered street,
> I call you by name, my green, my fluent mundo.[33]

He put his transferred passion for place most clearly in prose:

> One turns with something like ferocity toward a land that one
> loves, to which one is really and essentially native, to demand that
> it surrender, reveal, that in itself which one loves. This is a vital
> affair, not an affair of the heart (as it may be in one's first poems),
> but an affair of the whole being (as in one's last poems), an affair
> of fundamental life; so that one's cry of O Jerusalem becomes little
> by little a cry to something a little nearer and nearer until at last
> one cries out to a living name, a living place, a living thing, and

in crying out confesses openly all the bitter secretions of experience.[34]

But neither laments at spiritual deprivation nor hymns to its assuagement speak to lawyers specifically as lawyers. For that reason, I pass on to the question whether Stevens writes effectively of issues that are clearly relevant to law—social and political as well as personal alienation, economic as well as spiritual poverty. I agree with the consensus of critics, who think that even when he tries, Stevens does not succeed as a social or political poet.[35] He did attempt socially conscious poetry, during both world wars, and most notably during the Depression, partly in response to leftist critics' charges that his work, like the whole decadent Symbolist strand of modernism, was escapist and elitist—part of the social problem because not part of the solution.[36]

Stevens reacted to these criticisms with the longest poem he ever wrote, "Owl's Clover," an attempt to translate his own vague but agitated political stance into several hundred lines of blank verse.[37] Despite some effective passages, the poem as a whole was sufficiently unsuccessful that Stevens omitted it from his *Collected Poems.* He also wrote a number of shorter poems stimulated by the turmoil of the Depression, none of them among his best work.

The same can generally be said of Stevens's war poetry, the most ambitious of which is the long "Examination of the Hero in the Time of War," written in 1942.[38] Along with this latter poem, he issued a "Prose Statement" which expressed his poetic difficulty; in the presence of great external events, fact and its natural expression, journalism, overwhelmed his imagination. As he put it in a lecture given around the same time, the war, like the Depression, put too much "pressure of reality" on the poet in him; history had taken the form of "events" that were "beyond our power to reduce" and "metamorphose."[39] This explains a lot; after all, poetry (certainly Stevens's kind of poetry) *is* the imaginative reduction and metamorphosis of reality, and nothing could serve him as *materia poetica* that he could not seize and transform.

Stevens's one great poem on a public theme, in my opinion, is

the somber and beautiful war lyric "Death of a Soldier." Like a
leaf, "the soldier falls," and his

> Death is absolute and without memorial,
> As in a season of autumn,
> When the wind stops,
>
> When the wind stops and, over the heavens,
> The clouds go, nevertheless,
> In their direction.[40]

Stevens here treats the war not as a political phenomenon, an occasion for patriotic or pacifistic judgment, but (especially in the
pivotal and poignant "nevertheless") as a natural force, inexorable
as the change of seasons.

Stevens was part of the high modernist generation whose ideals
included that "religion of art" preached in its varied forms by
Schopenhauer and Nietzsche, Mallarmé and Pater, among others.
Science and positivistic philosophy had killed God but could not
fill the resulting spiritual void. The world was disenchanted; the
panther of the soul was locked in the industrial, technological,
and bureaucratic iron cage. Perhaps the artist held the key; perhaps poetry could bring release and reenchantment, a new kind of
Sunday morning.

But whose spirit was to be released? In the most hermetic version, it was to be only the poet's, who would go straight from the
iron cage to an ivory tower, there to distill a purified version of
the tribal language. Everything that smacked of mimesis, representation, content, meaning, message, the dull referential prose
of science was to be purged; poetry was to attain, so far as possible, the purely formal condition of music. Any audience for
such poetry would naturally be an elect few.

Competing with the formalist or decadent vision of pure poetry
was a conception drawn from social arts such as architecture, a
vision of poetry as ideally pervading and transforming the workaday industrial world. This vision, inherited from Emerson and
Whitman, preached in an English version by William Morris and

the arts-and-crafts movement, would later receive attractive defense in Dewey's *Art as Experience,* and undergo ultimate degradation in the theory and practice of Socialist Realism.[41] The debate continues today in the dispute between critics and defenders of the concept of High Culture and its traditional canon.[42]

Stevens was pulled in two directions on the question of poetic purity. His literary inclinations and the nature of his own talent drew him toward art for art's sake or pure poetry; at the same time, his American and democratic loyalties attracted him to the pervasive or populist version of modernism.[43] He mediated these conflicting impulses into a compromise that emerges, somewhat vaguely articulated, in essays and letters written during the thirties and forties.

On the side of purity, the poet had no obligations to address politically relevant topics. The ivory tower had to be available as a protected space for free creation, and the freedom it granted from political censorship had to extend as well to those poets whose temperament and talent drew them toward social and political themes, or toward relatively popular forms of expression.[44] On the other hand, there could be no *poésie pure* in the sense of form for its own sake, without concern for content.[45] The poet's source of inspiration was "his generation," and his role was to return to that generation something of what he derived from it. He should create poetry that would "help people lead their lives" by supplying them with a secular substitute for the dead gods— not poetry merely as decoration or exercise but as "a purging of the world's poverty and change and evil and death."[46]

These are great ambitions, but we still do not know what relation the poet's "help" to his fellow citizens will bear to politics and public affairs. On that subject, Richard Rorty in his recent *Contingency, Irony, and Solidarity* supplies a distinction useful for understanding Stevens's solution. Rorty argues, as a psychological theorist of law-and-literature (or politics-and-literature), that many literary writers are good at teaching morality—better than moral philosophers in most respects. But Rorty goes on to distinguish between two kinds of moral teaching: the private lessons

31

that help readers lead the good (individually fulfilling) life; and
the instruction, ethical in a stricter sense, that teaches them, by
increasing their capacity for imaginative identification, to treat
each other right.[47]

Rorty thus self-consciously makes the much-criticized liberal
distinctions between right and good, public and private morality.
A liberal himself, he insists that when lessons in soul building, as
taught for instance by Nietzsche and Heidegger, spill over into
the public realm, the results tend to be bad. Proust, by contrast,
is his example of a moral tutor who sticks to his strength, which
is showing how to make a satisfying work of art out of an individual life. Rorty's treatment is reminiscent of J. S. Mill's contrast
between Bentham as the better teacher of public policy and Coleridge as the better instructor in how to build a self.[48]

This public-private line cannot be drawn with any permanence
or precision, as is well illustrated by Mill's own uphill struggles
to define separate categories of "self-regarding" conduct and conduct potentially "harmful to others." The same point is made in
practice in every debate over liberal family and education policy—no rigorous political neutrality on questions of the good
character or the good life is finally possible. Still, I agree with
Rorty that some line defining and protecting a realm of tolera-
tion, privacy, and civil liberty must be drawn and defended (and
from time to time redrawn) if people are to have any hope of
maintaining a reasonably decent and free society in modern conditions.

Stevens, despite occasional lapses, mainly stuck to being an
effective teacher of the good private life. He shared the large faith
in the religion of art as his generation understood it—the belief
that the works of the imagination could heal the spiritual poverty
of individuals in a world left disenchanted by the unsuccessful
modern effort to replace God with science, industry, mass culture,
and bureaucracy. Many of his contemporaries—for example,
Yeats, Pound, and Eliot—carried their poetic religion into the
public arena and became aggressive opponents of liberalism,
which they considered the political representation of these sources

of contemporary disenchantment. Considering the alternatives they proposed, one must be thankful that they had little public influence. From my perspective, Stevens was less spectacularly wrong-headed in his politics than these other major poets of his time,[49] but still he had nothing inspiring or remarkable to say on public questions. Realizing this, he once wrote that a "time in which the poets' politics / Will rule in a poets' world" would come to pass only in a "world impossible for poets."[50]

He was also unsentimentally aware, as some current law-and-literature theorists do not seem to be, that the imagination does not always supply warmth, vitality, and humanity, and that reason is not always cold, mechanical, and unfeeling. Stevens came out of the remote and dandyist aesthetic tradition whose slogan was "Live? Our servants will do that for us."[51] Poets, he once wrote, "do not create in light and warmth alone"; they also create "in darkness and cold," and they may "create as the ministers of evil."[52] Poetry is "a destructive force" that "may kill a man."[53] It was his contemporary Walter Benjamin who said that "all efforts to render politics aesthetic culminate in one thing: war."[54] And Stevens well understood the romance of "evil made magic" through which suffering becomes spectacle and "the eye equates ten thousand deaths / With a single well-tempered apricot."[55]

In a late poem, Stevens took as his text Giovanni Papini's protest against the tendency of modern poets to retire from public poetry to their ivory towers as "the astute calligraphers of congealed daydreams, the hunters of cerebral phosphorescences." Papini asked, who was now to write "the hymn of victory or the psalm of supplication?" In response to this familiar interrogatory, Stevens pledged allegiance to "the heroic effort to live expressed / As victory." But he insisted that the modern poet, faced by contemporary "confusions of intelligence," could not simply chant "orotund consolations," but must struggle to "[accumulate] himself and time / For humane triumphals." Such poems would neither celebrate nor denounce the workable but uninspiring public institutions of the contemporary commercial republic or social democracy: "a politics / Of property is not an area / For triumphals." Rather (at least for the time being), the poet must gather his accumulations of self and time as he "sits and studies silence and himself." The resulting poems could then be "hymns appropriate to / The complexities of the world, when apprehended, / The intricacies of appearance, when perceived."[56]

In the classic critique already quoted, Walter Benjamin diagnosed fascism as the natural expression of political aestheticism—fascism that makes war, with its "fiery orchids of machine guns," into the goal of political activity. Benjamin was a great critic and literary theorist, but we should recall that the antidote he prescribed for the aestheticization of politics was communism, which responds "by politicizing art."[57] Stevens, cautiously bourgeois as ever, rejected both alternatives; given our experience with the practical implementation of Benjamin's prescription, who now seems the political naïf?

During the thirties, when it did seem that American poetry could have no agenda that was not communal and political, Stevens once gloomily remarked that he had made no contribution to society for which he might be remembered. An unlikely interlocutor with a longer view pulled him up short: "She reminded him of his poetry. Mrs. Stevens mentioned that his poetry would probably survive him."[58] She was right; he had the gift of being able to create for others, out of his own separation and loneliness, "by attentive thinking about concrete things, . . . an affectionate understanding of how good it was to be alive."[59] More than once, out of the bare ground of his sense of isolation and spiritual deprivation, he was able to raise his own triumphal hymn, to express the heroic effort to live as a kind of victory. But he had little to say—at least directly—about legal rights and duties, about the design of institutions, or even about how human beings should treat each other in those aspects of "private life" that are, because relational, also within the spheres of law and politics.

III

Fat Cat, Ghostly Rabbit

> It is difficult for a man whose whole life is thought to continue
> as a poet. The reason (like the law, which is only a form of the
> reason) is a jealous mistress.
>
> —Wallace Stevens, Letter to Barbara Church,
> September 29, 1952

> I believe in you my soul, the other I am must not abase itself to
>   you,
> And you must not be abased to the other.
>
> —Walt Whitman, "Song of Myself"

Can Wallace Stevens, poet, teach lawyers how to read and write better? Some law-and-literature proponents argue that law is essentially language, so that lawyers should be seen more as readers and writers than as social engineers, scientists, or philosophers. They thus become partisans in an old struggle, one that pitted the sophists against Plato, and the Roman rhetoricians against the jurisconsults—law as an art of persuasion, against law as a science of reason and analysis. One of the issues in the struggle is the kind of language that best and most honestly represents the process of legal judgment. Is it inevitably and desirably an open-ended and culturally embedded discourse that intertwines reason and emotion, or ideally a precise and impersonal logical calculus? This tends to mirror another, closely connected, dispute: Is law at its core a cultural practice of justification and legitimation, a form of ideology (hence properly rhetorical)? Or is it essentially coercive and imperative, a matter of rules and commands (to be expressed as clearly as possible)?

The aspiration to make law scientific has dominated legal

thought at least since the seventeenth century. This aspiration typically brings with it a conception of law as a set of coercive signals, ideally transmitted by a transparent and unambiguous medium. The primary function of legal language is then to represent factual information and portray logical operations or computations, on the basis of which state officials may exercise predictable coercive power and private individuals may plan their lives.

Under this view, the power of language to represent reality carries with it, inevitably, the power to misrepresent; and the kind of misrepresentation most significant in law is the rhetorical coloring of objective reality with subjective wishes and desires. Using rhetorical tropes and figures, a speaker can project emotions to an audience in the guise of objective qualities; the wished-for is transmuted into the desirable or just. To defend against such rhetorical distortion, the science-minded, whether they see legal science as a geometry of justice or as social engineering, urge the use of a plain unrhetorical style that keeps separate value and fact, subjective and objective, so that things may be portrayed as they are.

In the name of truth and clarity, Plato excluded verbal artificers such as sophists, poets, and dramatists from his ideal city; and rationalists, empiricists, and logical positivists have made an influential modern case for intellectualism and its linguistic guardian, the plain style. John Locke's familiar formulation of the case is representative, and was known to Wallace Stevens.[1] The tropes and figures of rhetoric, said Locke, bring "pleasure and delight," but because they conceal "things as they are," they should "in all discourses that pretend to inform or instruct perfectly . . . be avoided." Finally, "All the artificial and figurative applications of words eloquence hath invented, are for nothing else but to insinuate wrong *ideas,* move the passions, and thereby mislead the judgment, and so indeed are perfect cheat." Locke anticipates that rhetoric, fortified by the pleasure principle, will always have the advantage against "dry truth and real knowledge," for men "love to deceive and be deceived." In addition, he explicitly distinguishes the two styles by gender, foreseeing that his attempt to secure respect for "things as they are" will be thought masculine "brutality," because "eloquence, like the fair sex, has too prevailing beauties in it to suffer itself ever to be spoken against." [2]

Against the Lockean approach to language and the scientific world view, there has of course always been an opposition party. In ancient times and during the Renaissance, it consisted of the teachers and practitioners of the classical art of rhetoric; but since the nineteenth century, rhetoric has been supplanted by literature. Reacting to the triumphs of science and scientific philosophy during the Enlightenment, Romantics like Coleridge (whose American counterpart, using different terminology, was Emerson) proclaimed the imagination a mental faculty separate from and higher than the understanding, one that provided insight into a reality that is essentially vital and organic rather than static and mechanical. Imagination's champion was the creative artist, especially the writer, working through a language whose content was organically merged with its form: narrative, metaphor, poetry. [3]

In our own time, continuing the Romantic tradition, phenomenological, hermeneutic, and pragmatic approaches to social and legal theory have emphasized intuition, insight into meaning (*Verstehen*), and tacit belief as alternatives or supplements to the standard scientific account of the knowledge of human social life. Finally, from within the very capital of reason's empire has come the influential challenge (made by Thomas Kuhn and others) to the positivist account of natural science, stressing the role of imagination and persuasion, while downplaying that of proof or demonstration in scientific inquiry.

Contemporary legal thought, while largely dominated by analytical philosophy and law-and-economics, has its own counterparts to the Romantic resistance. The law-and-literature movement is merely one small part of a loose coalition of tendencies that depart from the traditional scientific model of inquiry, and from the view that legal language serves only to deceive whenever it does not transparently represent. The recent interpretive turn in legal scholarship has picked up from sociology and cultural anthropology a stress on the social construction of reality, the idea that law is, in Clifford Geertz's words, an important part of a culture's "distinctive manner of imagining the real"—an ideology or "*Anschauung* in the marketplace" and not just "a collection of ingenious devices to avoid disputes, advance interests, and adjust trouble-cases."[4] By these lights, law is ritual, drama, myth, and poetry more than social machinery; and in these cultural media, the substance and style cannot be cleanly separated, as they can in the scientific and mechanical model of law as regularized coercion.

Further, Locke's familiar division of language into its stern, workaday, literal, "masculine" side and its pleasant, diverting, figurative, "feminine" side has been taken up and turned around by recent feminist theorists. Indeed, they say, probably as a result of the gendered social division of labor, women are more adept at expressive and persuasive, as opposed to purely representational and imperative, uses of language. But as women enter the legal profession in increasing numbers, what has been a handicap for them may be an opportunity to correct the law's neglect of their qualities of insight, empathy, and interpersonal intuition as well their associated expressive, narrative, and metaphoric forms of language.[5] Members of other oppressed groups, racial and national, who have had little voice in the formation of law, take up the message; if they are to be included in the legal universe as full participants, the myths, songs, and stories that form the *nomoi* of their normative worlds must be given equal weight beside the reasonings of the philosophers and the findings of the social scientists.[6]

Finally, a number of legal scholars associated with the Critical Legal Studies movement have borrowed from linguistics and literary theory, and applied to law, a version of deconstructionism. Legal language, the critics argue, can only pretend to transparently transmit rules, commands, and justifications; inevitably it contains concealed contradictions and instabilities, which when revealed through deconstructive critique properly subvert the pretensions of lawyers, judges, and commentators to apolitical expertise and scientific objectivity.[7]

Law-and-literature advocates thus join culture interpreters and feminist, third-world, and deconstructionist critics in a loose coalition arrayed around the idea that lawyers and judges are or should be more like poets, storytellers, and interpreters than like scientists or engineers. The leading law-and-literature theorist, or antitheorist, James Boyd White, supplies some basic slogans: poetry teaches lawyers the negative capability to reconcile opposites (and adversaries) in the "comprehension of contrariety or contradiction";[8] poets merge the universal in the particular, the precept in the example, just as good common-law judges do; finally, poets both liberate and channel thought and conduct through trope, as judges preserve ordered liberty through the rule of (common) law.[9] Legal formalists and instrumentalists, who see law as geometry or as engineering, have not in this century faced so broadly assembled and well-articulated an opposition as they do today.

Can Wallace Stevens, poet and lawyer, speak for this coalition? It would seem that he might. As a poet, he rejected any notion that verbal style or form could be sharply distinguished from underlying content.[10] He also sometimes denied that his own legal and poetic worlds were incongruous: "One is not a lawyer one minute and a poet the next . . . I don't have a separate mind for legal work and another for writing poetry. I do each with my whole mind."[11] And he (at least once) articulated Professor White's comparison of poems and law cases: both unite the unique with the universal, embodying precept in example.[12]

Further, the central theme of Stevens's poetry, what he called "my reality-imagination complex,"[13] bears close kinship to the notion that reality is a social and linguistic construct—the notion that so dominates the law-and-literature attack on Locke's ideal of linguistic transparency. The scientific impulse to keep perception and computation of the real separate from mental play with the imaginary cannot be consistently carried through, the argument goes, because the basic conceptual and linguistic building blocks used in perception and computation originate in the collective social imagination; literal language largely consists of shared dead metaphor. Language can never be a transparent medium for the communication of reality, because reality is itself significantly constituted out of language. Stevens provides a number of oft-quoted aphoristic formulations of this position:

> It is a world of words to the end of it,
> In which nothing solid is its solid self. [14]

> The poem is the cry of its occasion,
> Part of the res and not about it.
> . . . . .
> Words of the world are the life of the world. [15]

>   Life consists
> Of propositions about life. [16]

In the opening canto of "Man with the Blue Guitar," Stevens plays Locke's phrase "things as they are" against "the blue guitar," symbol of the lyric imagination:

> They said, "You have a blue guitar,
> You do not play things as they are."

> The man replied, "Things as they are,
> Are changed upon the blue guitar."

> And they said then, "But play, you must,
> A tune beyond us, yet ourselves,

> A tune beyond the blue guitar
> Of things exactly as they are." [17]

We want reality played back to us, undistorted, in words, but nonlinguistic reality must be actively reduced and transformed in order to be represented linguistically; further, "things as they are" include human aspirations ("a tune beyond us, yet ourselves"), which are themselves generated and modified by poets, prophets, orators, advertisers, and other word-magicians. Stevens goes on to jingle the changes on the complex recursive relations between "things as they are" and "the blue guitar" throughout this long poem, providing a virtual anthem for the antiscientistic social (or legal) theorist.[18]

But the real question raised by the law-and-literature movement is not whether poets can supply anthems for legal theorists, but whether, as poets, they *are* themselves legal theorists, or authorities, or educators. Does their poetry as poetry speak to lawyers in some way in which its prose paraphrase cannot? Should lawyers and legal scholars modify their Lockean ideal of linguistic literality and transparence, conveying commands or predictions of the use of coercive force, to accommodate the metaphors and fables of rhetoricians and poets?

We can infer Stevens's negative answer to this question from both his preachment and his practice. He sharply differentiated the language of law from that of poetry, and, in his one unequivocal jurisprudential utterance, endorsed the related positivist view of law as organized coercion over the cultural theorists' view of it as legitimating ideology.

To take the linguistic point first: in his hours at the office, except for the moments he snatched from surety claims to devote to poetry, Stevens thought of himself as resting his blue guitar.[19] He emphatically distinguished between expository prose and poetry, speaking with displeasure of "the inability of a good many writers of prose to do their job: that is to say, to write prose." The essayist he was criticizing, Roger Caillois "doesn't write prose; he writes poetry that looks like prose. When it comes to thinking a thing out and to stating it simply, he seems invariably to evade direct thinking by lapsing into a metaphor or a parable and, in this way, he proves things, not by expressing reasons but by intimations to be derived from analogies."[20]

John Locke could not have made a more emphatic distinction between expository prose and poetry. And Stevens as lawyer implemented the Lockean ideal of prosaic transparency with a rigor that won him renown in his own working circle. His legal writing was concise, stripped-down, unadorned, and remarkably direct. One legal colleague "loved his letters. He'd . . . say yes or no, and that was it. When it came to business, he didn't mince words."[21] According to A. J. Fletcher, a field attorney who handled cases for the Hartford, Stevens's instruction letter transmitting the case was invariably so accurate and comprehensive that no reference back for further instructions was necessary; the style of the letters was "clear, and concise, and beautiful."[22] Another field lawyer summed it up: "You felt you were dealing with a superintellect. In the many exchanges we had over the years—letters—I always had the feeling that here was a man that could get right down to the nub of the matter."[23]

Stevens's only departure from the plain style was the occasional foray into decorative figure, mostly in letters to colleagues who were also friends, and who cherished references like the one to an opposing lawyer's smile as being "like the silver plate on a coffin," and the one to an inadequate settlement as revealing "how the hippopotamus felt when someone threw him a handful of raspberries."[24] Most of Stevens's legal correspondence has been discarded, but his expository style is apparent in an article he wrote for an insurance journal describing the work of the surety lawyer, and in those among his published personal letters that come closest to being legal advice or argument. They are indeed, as reported, direct, analytic, and attractively plain in style.[25]

The transparency Stevens sought and achieved in legal writing was of course no part of his poetry, which, especially in the poems of *Harmonium,* attains the "essential gaudiness" he sought. This is the poet whose "moonlight / Fubbed the girandoles," whose "disaffected flagellants . . . smacked their muzzy bellies," whose "silentious porpoises . . . dibbled in waves that were mustachios;" who sang of "futura's fuddle-fiddling lumps," enjoyed "ithy oonts and long-haired / Plomets," and commanded: "Chieftan Iffucan of Azcan in caftan / Of tan with henna hackles, halt!"[26]

A number of Stevens's work colleagues, impressed by the clarity and directness of his legal writing, were amazed when they tried to read his poetry. Thus Charles O'Dowd: "His letters were as clear and precise as his poetry was obtuse—at least, obtuse to me."[27] And to Clifford Burdge, the gap was so great that Stevens seemed to him "a kind of sane schizophrenic": Stevens had "two compartments in his mind, poetry and law," from the latter of which emerged "beautifully lucid legal writing" while from the other came incomprehensible verse.[28]

If Burdge had looked at Stevens's prose essays on poetics, he would have been equally baffled; their language (in the terms Stevens applied critically to Caillois) characteristically "evades direct thinking" by its resort to "metaphor and parable." Here, for example, is Stevens expanding on a statement of poetic "realism," the thesis that "the accuracy of accurate letters is an accuracy with respect to the structure of reality":[29]

What the eye beholds may be the text of life. It is, nevertheless, a text that we do not write. The eye does not beget in resemblance. It sees. But the mind begets in resemblance as the painter begets in representation; that is to say, as the painter makes his world within a world; or as the musician begets in music, in the obvious small pieces having to do with gardens in the rain or the fountains of Rome and in the obvious larger pieces having to do with the sea, Brazilian night or those woods in the neighborhood of Vienna in which the hunter was accustomed to blow his horn and in which, also, yesterday, the birds sang preludes to the atom bomb.[30]

Why does Stevens write this way? The poet, as Stevens remarked of one of Paul Valéry's prose dialogues, naturally avoids being "explicit as to his real conception, which he likes to suggest or imply, not state."[31] Not only the poem itself but the poet's prose explanations of his creative process "must resist the intelligence almost successfully."[32] As the poet approaches his creative center, his thought "makes itself manifest in a kind of speech that comes from secrecy. Its position is always an inner position, never certain, never fixed."[33] Too much self-consciousness, too much analytic clarity, threatens poetic creativity; the poet must respect the "foundling of the infected past" that lives in the rag and bone shop of the imagination:

> . . . look not at his colored eyes. Give him
> No names. Dismiss him from your images.
> The hot of him is purest in the heart.[34]

Stevens often distinguished between opposed realms of poetry ("the mundo of the imagination") and philosophy ("the gaunt world of reason").[35] And he identified law with philosophy, as part of the world of reason. As he said of his old mentor George Santayana, who had turned from poetry to philosophy: "The reason (like the law, which is only a form of the reason) is a jealous mistress," so that one whose whole life is thought will find it hard "to continue as a poet."[36] Or, as he put it to another correspondent in 1940, "a poet has got to preserve feeling and . . . thinking has a way of clearing up things from which feeling commonly arises: there is an antipathy between thinking and feeling."[37] Remarks like these reflect only one side of Stevens's complex view on the place of thought in poetry (I will seek to correct the imbalance later), but it was this side that was at work in separating his legal from his poetic writing and thinking styles.

One of Stevens's strangest poems, and one of his own favorites, shows him separating his after-hours imaginative-poetic self from his workaday prose-reason-money self to a degree that almost warrants an unqualified attribution of split personality. "A Rabbit as King of the Ghosts" begins with a sentence fragment evoking the waning of sunlight and reason at dusk:

> The difficulty to think at the end of day,
> When the shapeless shadow covers the sun
> And nothing is left except light on your fur—

With night, the rabbit's fur is lit by the moon, symbol of the imagination; this is an unreal world sharply distinct from the daytime, where another animal reigned:

> There was the cat slopping its milk all day,
> Fat cat, red tongue, green mind, white milk
> And August the most peaceful month.

The fat practical cat's colors, blood red and grass green, are for
Stevens standard symbols of reality, "things as they are."

The rabbit, somehow both Caliban and Ariel, likes it as night
falls and the moon spreads its indefinite light:

> To be, in the grass, in the peacefullest time,
> Without that monument of cat,
> The cat forgotten in the moon;
>
> And to feel that the light is a rabbit-light,
> In which everything is meant for you
> And nothing need be explained;
>
> Then there is nothing to think of.

The imagination has its time of triumph, as the day's prosy distinctions are obliterated, and subject blends into object:

> It comes of itself;
> And east rushes west and west rushes down,
> No matter. The grass is full
>
> And full of yourself. The trees around are for you,
> The whole of the wideness of night is for you,
> A self that touches all edges,
>
> You become a self that fills the four corners of night.

As the imagination's expansion becomes increasingly alarming,
the poet apostrophizes the rabbit, formerly timid and fuzzy in the
daylight, now exulting in its after-hours omnipotence, painting,
repainting, and miniaturizing its feline adversary:

> The red cat hides away in the fur-light
> And there you are humped high, humped up,
>
> You are humped higher and higher, black as stone—
> You sit with your head like a carving in space
> And the little green cat is a bug in the grass. [38]

As in other Stevens poems, when imagination runs so free as to
reduce reality to a little bug in the grass, madness threatens; [39] but

for this poem at least, the poet's sympathy is with the crazy rabbit against the sane and efficient cat.

A letter Stevens wrote in 1928, during a period of hard work at the office and of poetic sterility, helps gloss the milk-and-moonlight contrast of this remarkable poem. Explaining an earlier poem's insistence on the need for contact with reality, Stevens writes: "After writing a poem, it is a good thing to walk round the block; after too much midnight, it is pleasant to hear the milkman." Too much undiluted imagination can make a poet as unbalanced as that night-filling rabbit; some relief is necessary. But the poem Stevens was glossing had concluded with a famous apostrophe to the rabbit's side: "Unreal, give back to us what once you gave: / The imagination that we spurned and crave."[40] His correspondent had evidently asked how to reconcile this with the poem's earlier insistence on maintaining contact with reality. Stevens's answer was unequivocal: while the milkman supplies necessary relief, still, "and this is the point of the poem, the imaginative world is the only real world after all."[41]

The law and its prose were separate from poetry, and supplied a form of relief for Stevens by way of contrast with poetry, as the milkman relieves from the moonlight, as the walk around the block relieves the writer's trancelike absorption. But the priority was clear: imagination, poetry, and secrecy, pursued after hours, were primary, good in themselves; reason, prose, and clarity, indulged in during working hours, were secondary and instrumental. As Stevens wrote to his daughter when she wanted to leave college to make her own way (and he spoke as a man past sixty, with a lifetime of experience), "None of the great things of life have anything to do with making your living."[42]

Stevens had established this relation between the world of prose and poetry, reason and imagination, early in his life. In 1899, while he was still in college, he noted in his journal that the poet uses "study as a contrast to poetry." It provides "a place to spring from—a refuge from the heights, an anchorage of thought." Study "ties you down," and only "the occasional wilful release from this voluntary bond . . . gives the soul its occasional over-powering sense of lyric freedom and effort."[43]

Study was thus the milkman; poetry, the moonlight. Stevens would later establish this very relation between his own mentally demanding legal work and his poetry, keeping distinct their styles of thought, feeling, and writing. He spoke of the "pleasure" of the "habitual, customary" that he took in his job; it was "the normality of the normal," a "solid rock under his feet."[44] "I love the office," he said in another letter. "We call the office the rockpile, yet so large a rockpile is a good deal more than that."[45]

Stevens would ultimately make the routine pleasures of ordinary work the theme of one of the central passages in his poetry. In "Notes toward a Supreme Fiction" (III, viii), he spoke, as he seldom did, in the first person; and in lines that are among his most famous, he portrayed the imagination's power in an angel's Miltonic plunge through the abyss of space, concluding, "I have not but I am and as I am, I am." Characteristically, he immediately qualified the affirmation: however glorious, this was an imaginary angel, moonshine, "Cinderella fulfilling herself beneath a roof." And in the next canto, Stevens alternated milkman with moonshine, praising the domestic chirpings of a robin, which, though "mere repetitions,"

> . . . at least comprise
> An occupation, an exercise, a work,
>
> A thing final in itself and, therefore, good:
> One of the vast repetitions final in
> Themselves and, therefore, good, the going round,
>
> And round and round, the merely going round,
> Until merely going round is a final good,
> The way wine comes at a table in a wood.[46]

The last line reminds us that Stevens's milkman, his job at the Hartford, had another, more instrumental function: wine must be paid for. "I like Rhine wine, blue grapes, endive and lots of books, etc., etc., etc., as much as I like supreme fiction," he wrote to his rich friend Henry Church, explaining why he was quite willing to leave his poetic projects in abeyance during the working day.[47] The Hartford supported Stevens and his family in a style to which few serious poets are able to become accustomed.

Stevens's friend and business colleague Wilson Taylor has said that while Stevens was a conscientious and effective lawyer and executive, his only real motive for work was economic.[48] But milk as a refreshing alternative to moonlight may have been as real a need for Stevens. He stayed at his job long past retirement age, possibly past the time he needed the money, and turned down the Norton lectureship in poetry at Harvard because a prolonged absence might have led the company to replace him.[49] He continued to work on *"because I like to do so* and have use for the money, and I never had any other reasons for doing so."[50]

Stevens's "use for the money," though, went beyond buying blue grapes, leather-bound books, and the other luxuries to which he was attached. He had a wife to support, as well as a divorced daughter to help out, and, ironically for an insurance executive, was prevented by high blood pressure from obtaining the life insurance through which he could have guaranteed their security.[51] This suggests a third motive, less entirely instrumental than refreshment and money, for Stevens's devotion to his job, and ultimately for his keeping the kind of writing it involved sharply separate from his poetry: male self-esteem. Recall Locke's separation of the masculine truth-preserving prose of reason from the feminine pleasure-giving figuration of poetry and rhetoric; this reminds us that, at least in the United States (Locke's country as much as God's), poetry is not considered an occupation for a real man.[52]

When Stevens started collecting his early poems with an eye to publication, he wrote to his wife: "Keep this all a great secret. There is something absurd about all this writing of verses . . . My habits are positively lady-like."[53] Stevens's father had early impressed on him that the question facing the American male is: "Starting with nothing, how shall I sustain myself and perhaps a wife and family—and send my boys to College and live comfortably in my old age."[54] The warning was clear: poetry writing is all right after hours, but first, earn a manly living. A year later, Wallace was worrying in his journal about those who "say poetry is now the peculiar province of women"; they could be refuted if poets would write like "Homer, Dante, Shakespeare, Milton, Keats, Browning, much of Tennyson—they are your man poets." Later, as his own verse developed in the direction that would make critics call him decorative, escapist, exotic, anything but virile and central, this fear of emasculation continued to trouble him.[55]

But despite all the pressures of background and environment, Stevens managed largely to stay faithful to the bent of his own genius toward an androgynous poetry of receptivity and multiple perspectives. Apart from occasional aberrations toward virile war heroes and Nietzschean supermen, he eschewed the masculine poetry of forceful statement or plain language, and developed his naturally playful, indirect, and often exotic style.

Stevens's androgynous tendency sometimes extended beyond his diction or style to perspective, as he from time to time portrayed a woman as the poetic creator rather than as muse or love-object, or even identified his voice directly as female. Thus, it is the beach-striding woman singer who imposes order on the tumultuous sea in "The Idea of Order at Key West." And in "The World as Meditation," Stevens speaks as an earth-Penelope whose fertile patience leaves on the margin the wandering male sun-Ulysses. Finally, in a decisive late self-representation ("Final Soliloquy of the Interior Paramour"),[56] he speaks in the voice of a female, no longer the silently inspiring muse, who has actually at last absorbed her poet.

Stevens was able to defuse his sexual anxiety and preserve his authentically androgynous poetic voice in this way by marking out an inviolate sphere of unquestioned masculinity in his working life. His colleague Herbert Schoen said: "Actually, Wallace Stevens was proud of this facet of his life . . . He was very proud that he earned his living—and it was a good living—that he did it on his own; and that he did it separately and apart from his writing of poetry."[57] The job was, then, "separate and apart" from poetry in every way. It was a man's work, distinct from universities and the lecture circuit, and it involved the traditionally masculine business of law and big money.[58] In that work, Stevens's large body, clothed in an expensive plain suit, topped by an imposing head and close-cropped hair, made him an impressively patriarchal figure. At the same time, against the barriers of his shyness and natural reticence, he pressed ahead to seem one of the boys, part of the all-male crowd that ate lunch, drank together, and cracked jokes at the Canoe Club.[59] The work also allowed him to fulfill the traditional American male role of family support that his father had so forcefully impressed on him.[60] Finally, and what is relevant to this study, he accepted, mastered, and made his own, at the office, the plain unadorned working style certified as masculine at least since John Locke.*

As one aspect of the separation he imposed between his poetic and legal worlds, Stevens scarcely ever mentioned law in his poetry or his lectures on poetics. One of the rare exceptions came at the beginning of his lecture "Imagination as Value," where he discussed Pascal's claim that "the chancellor is grave and clothed with ornaments, for his position is unreal . . . Judges, physicians, etc., appeal only to the imagination."[61] Stevens remarked that if in fact law and order could be established "merely by dressing a few men in uniforms," this would be not an evil but a "potent good."[62] No revolutionary he.

But for our purposes, I want to leave aside whether he thought it a good or bad thing that legal authority should be a social and rhetorical construct, manufactured out of uniforms, ermine robes, high-sounding formulas, and ideologies of justice. Our question is whether he accepted Pascal's account of the rhetorical and imaginative basis of legal authority. If he did, we can enlist him among those who treat law primarily as language, ritual, and drama, rather than as the organized application of collective coercion.

---

*Late in life Stevens remarked: "I always used to think that I got my practical side from my father, and my imagination from my mother;" (Jerald Hatfield, "More about Legend," *Trinity Review*, 8 [May 1954]: 30) Similarly, Judge Posner, who urges that "the literary should be a sphere apart" from the legal, dedicated his *Law and Literature* to "my mother, who initiated me into the pleasures of literature, and my father, who urged me to go to law school."

In fact, Stevens did not accept this view. "Pascal knew perfectly well that the chancellor had force behind him."[63] It was force that made him a chancellor rather than a preacher or a poet. As might be expected of one who in his own life insisted on separating the rabbit's imagined land of poetry from the cat's "real" world of law, business, and power, he proclaimed himself a scientific legal positivist, finding the essence of law not in the substance or the packaging of its claims to legitimacy, but in its deployment of coercive power. The stern legal theory fit with the spare legal style of a lawyer-poet who said that "the style of men and men themselves are one."[64] But which style—the legal or the poetic—was one with the man who wrote both Stevens's poetry and his legal letters of instruction?

IV

Steel against Intimation

Reality is a cliché from which we escape by metaphor.

—Wallace Stevens, "Adagia"

Trace the gold sun about the whitened sky
Without evasion by a single metaphor.
Look at it in its essential barrenness
And say this, this is the centre that I seek.

—Wallace Stevens, "Credences of Summer"

So far, the teaching from Stevens's practice and preaching is Judge Posner's: law and literature are, and should be, worlds apart. Law is law by virtue of the force that stands behind the chancellor. And because law is force regularized, the purpose of its rules is to signal clearly when that force will be deployed. Law's primary linguistic virtue is thus the absence of ambiguity—the opposite of much good poetry, and certainly of Stevens's own.

Once, at a symposium on "Law and the Humanities," I heard a Stevens poem turn in the direction of this doctrinal point—but then, being a Stevens poem, it kept turning toward its own qualification. The symposium began with James Boyd White's giving his "poetic" conception of law study as one of the humanities rather than as a would-be social science, and law practice as skillful reading and writing rather than social engineering. Margaret Jane Radin responded, declining the choice thus posed between scientific and humanistic models of law, and proposing a third, pragmatist, alternative.

The pragmatist, she suggested, sees law as practice, as institutionalized action in problematic situations—a view that requires an oscillation between perspectives. On the one hand, legal judg-

ment is indeed linguistically and culturally rooted: looking backward, it is guided by rule or precept within a shaping tradition
and context that require interpretation. But legal judgment also
looks forward to results, aiming at social ends outside itself. The
exclusively textual and hermeneutic emphasis of law-and-literature scholarship tends to submerge the instrumental perspective,
and so diverts attention from the crude and often violent nonver-
bal consequences of legal decision. Professor Radin concluded by
reading Stevens's "The Motive for Metaphor," which (heard in the
context of her talk) contrasts a nuanced literary and imaginary
world of metaphor with a harsh and literal real world:

> You like it under the trees in autumn,
> Because everything is half dead.
> The wind moves like a cripple among the leaves
> And repeats words without meaning.
>
> In the same way, you were happy in spring,
> With the half colors of quarter-things,
> The slightly brighter sky, the melting clouds,
> The single bird, the obscure moon—
>
> The obscure moon lighting an obscure world
> Of things that would never be quite expressed,
> Where you yourself were never quite yourself
> And did not want nor have to be,
>
> Desiring the exhilarations of changes:
> The motive for metaphor, shrinking from
> The weight of primary noon,
> The A B C of being,
>
> The ruddy temper, the hammer
> Of red and blue, the hard sound—
> Steel against intimation—the sharp flash,
> The vital, arrogant, fatal, dominant X.[1]

The poem seems to override the fragile "intimation" of language
and imagination with the "steel" of force—a caution against the
"motive for metaphor" that may tempt us to see reality (including

law) as merely imagery, dialogue, and discourse. I agree that this point is in the poem, but have come to see a submerged secondary meaning in it as well, one that brings the deliberate ambiguities of poetry's metaphors to the vital and dominant center of things.

The crux or pivot of "The Motive for Metaphor" is its title phrase, which appears at the beginning of the fourth stanza, where the poem swings from the autumn-spring world of metaphor to the world of "primary noon" and its "dominant X." The world of metaphor is unified around change and obscurity: qualities positive in the spring of youth, but decadent in autumn. The appealing phenomena that made us happy in spring—light, clouds, bird, and moon—were the "*half* colors of *quarter*-things." It was fractionation and incompletion that we liked, and the natural beauties corresponded to the happiness of open-ended potential: a world not fully expressible because full of feelings, a self not yet finally defined and thus without known limits. In autumn, we less enthusiastically "like it . . . / Because everything is *half* dead"—attractive only by comparison with the approaching alternative. Now the fact of mutability points us not vitally toward summer's prime but fatally toward winter.

Obscurity, like incompletion, is shared by spring and autumn. The spring moon was, we hear twice, "obscure," and lighted an "obscure world" of "things that would never be quite expressed," while the crippled autumn wind "repeats words without meaning." Again, a quality that was positive in spring has become negative in autumn.

Metaphor combines change and obscurity. It transforms our view of its focal subject by viewing it through a novel frame; at the same time, its figuration tends to create a riddle or an obscurity by contrast with the clarity of literal speech. Metaphor is at home both in spring and autumn by virtue of these two qualities, but with contrasting connotations in the two seasons:

> Desiring the exhilarations of changes:
> The motive for metaphor, shrinking from
> The weight of primary noon . . .

54

We were drawn to metaphor in spring by desire for excitement, but now in autumn by fear of reality.

The first three stanzas, with the contrasting positive (spring) and negative (autumn) connotations they give to change, obscurity, and metaphor, use verb tenses to fix their overall evaluative tone: autumn is now, spring is past. This brings us to the last two stanzas' world of primary noon expecting fixity, clarity, and literality, and ready to see these qualities in a positive light. What we find is a workplace, a forge, where fire imparts a ruddy temper to metal, which the smith shapes decisively with his steel hammer, amid hard sounds and sparks, before it cools and fixes into final form. This is the poem's reality, "the vital, arrogant, fatal, dominant X."

If we are viewing the poem in jurisprudential terms, the practical workplace imagery can return us to Stevens's own daytime workplace, where lawyer-insurers hammered out their blunt repairs to the commercial world's mishaps. The smith's steel hammer (striking while the iron is hot) represents both law's force and the lawyer's virtue of decisive judgment unambiguously expressed. We recall Stevens's view that steely power, more than rhetorical and ritual intimations of legitimacy, is what gives legal judgments their authority. The sun's "weight of primary noon" suggests the law's pitiless scrutiny,[2] and the "A B C of being" connotes the plain, unpoetic, and literal language in which the world's real business is conducted, by real men, who, in Justice Holmes's phrase, "think things, not words."[3]

Though we may doubt whether Stevens himself thought of the poem mainly in these legal terms, he certainly did mean it as one of his recurrent meditations on the relation between imagination and reality. Of the two dialectical partners, this poem favors reality—at least on first impression—and expresses Stevens's fear that metaphor (and the kind of *symboliste* poetry that is identified with metaphor) represents a morally ambivalent flight into fantasy.

Placing the poem in its context in Stevens's life strengthens this reading. From the Depression of the 1930s onward, Stevens's letters, and to a lesser degree his poems and lectures, were filled with his yearning to touch the central concerns of a wider audience. He reported feeling "isolated" and "on the edge" as a poet, and spoke of his need to move in his writing toward the "central," the "normal," to "share the common life," all of which he associated with "reality."[4] In the letter I have just been quoting, written in 1940, he identified the "center" with "a photograph of a lot of fat men and women in the woods, drinking beer and singing Hi-li Hi-lo"; he was convinced that he "ought to try to achieve" this "normal" in his poetry.[5] In 1946, Stevens again stated this theme in the strongest terms: "For myself, the inaccessible jewel is the normal and all of life, in poetry, is the difficult pursuit of just that," and in 1948, echoing "The Motive for Metaphor," he wrote that a "poet writes of twilight because he shrinks from noonday."[6]

Stevens's distaste for the "shrinking" aspects of his nature was particularly troubling to him in 1942, when he wrote "The Motive for Metaphor."[7] In a lecture given that year, he spoke of the poet's mission to "help people live their lives." Yet, he asked in Shakespeare's words, "How with this rage can beauty hold a plea?" His since much-quoted answer was that poetry serves "self-preservation" by supplying "a violence within that protects us from the violence without." During the war, there could be little doubt what was the particular "rage" and "violence without" that Stevens meant. But the same lecture shows how deeply he doubted his capacity to supply the antidote; he described shrinking from the plain or definite poetic portrayal of "nobility" as from something "false and dead and ugly," something that produced "shame" and "horror" in the "sensitive poet, conscious of negations."[8]

Earlier that year he had published "Notes toward a Supreme Fiction," and to that most unwarlike and untopical masterpiece he had appended a curious Coda that, in its awkward striving to link his poetry to martial and popular concepts of nobility, illustrated his problem. At his insistence, some lines from this Coda were even printed on the book jacket.[9] The Coda proclaims the interdependence of the soldier's actual war and the poet's own never-ending "war between the mind / And sky." The two wars are said to be "one . . . a plural, a right and left, a pair, / Two parallels that meet," if only in "a book in a barrack, a letter from Malay." The soldier, whose war will end though the poet's continues, is said to be "poor without the poet's lines." Indeed the closing tercet celebrates "how simply," with the aid of the poet's ministrations, "the fictive hero becomes the real" and "How gladly with proper words the soldier dies, / If he must, or lives on the bread of faithful speech." [10]

Whatever note this may have struck in 1942, today it sounds pretentious and offensive, unworthy of the great poem to which it is appended. Stevens is neither a Kiplingesque barrackroom bard nor a Whitmanian wound-dresser; his language is as different as possible from "the bread of faithful speech" in which ordinary soldiers or their loved ones could have found sustenance. [11] The "parallels" he finds between his metaphoric "war" with the blank page and the soldier's bloody war seem apologetic, forced, even ludicrous. He fails utterly to surmount the barriers raised by Wilfred Owen and other twentieth-century war poets against home-front verse that supplies proper words for soldiers to die by. [12]

The context supplied by Stevens's Depression and wartime anxieties about his marginality (the legislative history for the work of our unacknowledged legislator) casts a lunar light on the question whether to read "The Motive for Metaphor" in jurisprudential terms. On the one hand, it suggests that Stevens did associate the autumn-spring land of metaphor with the obscurity and escapist tendencies of his poetry, and noonday with the "centrality" and "normality" of the real world of action, power, and public common life. His own real daytime world was the world of law and insurance, which we know he identified with the clear businesslike prose of his own professional writing. We also know that Stevens thought law was more steel than intimation ("The chancellor has force behind him"), and some readers have found a guillotine as well as a forge in the poem's noonday scene.

On the other hand, Stevens was probably concerned more with the war effort than with his workaday world of law and business as his primary reference for "reality" in 1942. The two were not unconnected; Hartford surety bonds covered defense contracts during the war. And Stevens, perhaps not incidentally, avoided the central role in corporate policy his colleagues wished him to play during this period—presumably so as to reserve time and energy for writing.[13] Still, the main war effort to which Stevens felt so unhappily marginal was probably the writing of central poetry that might inspire or console his fellow citizens. He seems to have wished that he could strike poetic sparks of "red [white] and blue" with his poet's hammer.[14] Perhaps he thought that if volumes of verse were found in the barracks, they were more likely to be by Robert Frost than by Wallace Stevens.[15] A few years later he would note in a letter that Ireland had sent a battleship to bring the body of Yeats home as a national hero; he knew that he would never be that kind of public poet.[16]

But even if Stevens himself had war rather than law mainly in mind as the external reference of the noontime world portrayed in "Motive," he would not have regarded this as excluding a jurisprudential reading—if the reading fit.[17] At the same time he would also, however reluctantly for so reticent a man, have invited the reader's attention to the human context that is the shadowy spirit to the carnal letter of every text.[18] Here that context at least intimates law as one possible referent for the poem's workplace, that harshly dominant and fatal but vital reality. Stevens saw law, like war, as politics carried on by other means; he saw both in terms ultimately of force, and both could well stand in for the kind of reality to which he felt so marginal in 1942.[19]

If we apply the poem to present-day schools of legal thought, one "motive for metaphor" is the legal humanist's desire for "the exhilarations of changes"—the excitement of transmuting the base metal of law's crude raw material into art. The darker, autumnal side of this motive is its "shrinking" from law's noontime realities of prisons and money, pain and greed, into the more sheltered and congenial domain of texts, tropes, and dialogue. The civilized view of law as cultured conversation unduly neglects the "hard sound" of "steel against intimation," the sound of force against eloquence, sharp blades against the soft flesh of the human bodies that, more than any words, should be the lawyer's first concern. On this reading, "The Motive for Metaphor" cleanly separates—as Stevens did in his life, and as Judge Posner tells us we should do in our legal scholarship—the realms of poetry and law, shadow and sunlight, the rabbit and the cat.

But while the poem seems to me to bear this reading, it does more as well, and in so doing partly undoes what it did. Recall that the common elements of the poem's spring-autumn world were change or incompletion on the one hand, and obscurity on the other. These elements, attractive in the spring of youth, less so now in autumnal maturity, were identified with metaphor, commonly conceived as a trope both transformative and obscure relative to literal speech.

These qualities of metaphoricity, change, and obscurity in the poem's moonlit autumn-spring world prepare us to find in its conclusion literality, stability, and clarity; and indeed the first images meet our expectations: "The motive for metaphor, shrinking from / The weight of primary noon, / The A B C of being." "Primary noon" suggests the clear, and "A B C of being" the literal. But at the same time, noon is said to have "weight," an obvious metaphor, and then in the last stanza the metaphors for reality become particularly obtrusive:

> The ruddy temper, the hammer
> Of red and blue, the hard sound—
> Steel against intimation—the sharp flash,
> The vital, arrogant, fatal, dominant X.

The metaphoric sequence of hammer, steel, hard sound, and flash culminate in X, that "ultimate metaphor, never quite itself and always ready to assume another identity."[20] Now, if we look back, we can see that the expected contrast is really present in reverse: the opening two lines of the poem ("You like it under the trees in autumn / Because everything is half dead") are unusually flat and literal for Stevens, and after the figure of wind as muttering cripple in the next couplet, the portrayal of spring in stanzas two and three is itself plain and relatively unfigurative.[21]

So much for literality. What about clarity? The concluding series of imagistic phrases in apposition—at least most of them—do refer to a forge or smithy. The tenor of this metaphor does indeed seem to be reality; but without further explanation, *reality* is one of the most obscure of concepts. What aspect of reality is meant? The exceptional and violent world of war? The workaday world of earning a living? A poetry that goes beyond the easy play of youthful obscurity to express mature commitment? (In a 1940 poem, Stevens had written: "The prologues are over. It is a question, now, / Of final belief . . . It is time to choose.")[22] Further, what are we to make of the parenthetical phrase "steel against intimation"? What can "intimation" represent in a smithy? Far from answering any of these questions, the poem ends in oracular obscurity: "the . . . X." Nor do the elided adjectives resolve anything; life ("vital") is set against death ("fatal"), leaving an algebraic variable that we may indeed experience as both "arrogant" and "dominant" in its sphinxlike challenge: solve for X.

Instead of literality, metaphor; instead of clarity, obscurity—what, then, of our expectation that we might find stability in the real world of the last stanzas? This expectation, too, is frustrated: the only fixity to be found there, the hardening of the heated metal, will come later if at all; the actual scene is one of frantically rapid transformation, and the associated images—the quickly fading glow of heated metal, the sparks, the flash, the "hard sound"—all evoke the transitory. And the poem's metaphoric temporal frame speeds up, from the slow passage of the seasons (spring, autumn) to the fleeting of a single day; reality appears not as the summer we expect, but only as the moment of noon.[23]

What are we to make of this paradox, the poem's turn in the final stanzas toward metaphor, the obscure, the transitory, where we were led to expect the literal, clear, and stable? Habitual Stevens readers can anticipate the answer: this reflexive and self-questioning poet's "reality-imagination complex" is always just that, a complex intertwining, never a neat schema. The only certainty is that a Stevens poem that starts by equating metaphor with the obscure-transitory-unreal and the literal with the clear-stable-real will not continue by simply charting out these binary oppositions in all their classic symmetry.

"Motive" appeared in *Transport to Summer*, a book title whose wordplay suggests the point behind the poem's reversal.[24] Summer in Stevens, like noon, represents reality; metaphor is the figure of movement, of carrying across, of transport (you can ride a literal *metaphora*, the public bus, in Athens today). The volume contains a number of poems about the relation of metaphor to reality, a topic of abiding interest to Stevens. As well as being a suspicious critic of this "evasive" trope, he also joined in the Romantic celebration of what Shelley called poetry's "vitally metaphoric" power to carry its readers to a new revelation of an ever-changing reality.[25]

Metaphor's obscurity, as well as its dynamic quality, is part of this power. The sunlit visible is not the whole of reality, so the Romantic tradition insists; there is an unseen world missed by those who attend only to the clear and distinct, relying solely on healthy eyes and transparent prose.[26] Stevens often uses sound, especially inarticulate sound, to represent aspects of reality that most resist prose description; in this trope, he turns from the sunlight to the shaded woods in order to avoid visual distraction, in order to open his ears to the faint sounds and the still, small voice. Thus, in "The Creations of Sound" (1944), Stevens criticizes a poet named "X" who fails to make "the visible a little hard to see"; the Stevensian poet clouds vision not to hide reality, but to make audible the real, though invisible, "second part of life," the "syllables that rise / From the floor, rising in speech we do not speak."[27] In other poems, the opposition is between high-pitched chatter and deeper, wordless sound; the injunction in any case is to hear sounds from the side of being that escapes our distracted everyday (visually dominated) attention.[28]

In this way, poetic obscurity (and metaphor) can actually serve reality. Stevens speaks not for an aesthetic of mystification but rather on behalf of a kind of realism, in his oft-quoted first sentence of "Man Carrying Thing": "The poem must resist the intelligence / Almost successfully." He continues:

> Illustration
>
> A brune figure in winter evening resists
> Identity. The thing he carries resists
>
> The most necessitous sense. Accept them, then,
> As secondary (parts not quite perceived
>
> Of the obvious whole, uncertain particles
> Of the certain solid, the primary free from doubt,
>
> Things floating like the first hundred flakes of snow
> Out of a storm we must endure all night,
>
> Out of a storm of secondary things),
> A horror of thoughts that suddenly are real.
>
> We must endure our thoughts all night, until
> The bright obvious stands motionless in cold.[29]

In this poem, at dusk, with snow starting to fall, an indistinct "brune figure," carrying something likewise indistinct, appears outside. The figure with its object resists "the most necessitous sense," sight, and thus resists "identity"—it is not quite itself. This figure, dimly seen and designated by the obscure word "brune," is like a difficult poem or an opaque metaphor carrying a less than obvious meaning; it represents a "secondary" reality apart from the visible, the "primary free from doubt." Speculating on what it may be (a burglar? a homeless person? a dead poet returned from Hades?)[30] brings a horrifying storm of suddenly real thoughts that last until morning, when the "bright obvious stands motionless in cold."

The "bright obvious" may be a harmless and banal external figure (a snowman with a broom?), or it may be a stark vision of a previously evaded reality ("motionless" suggests death) congealed out of the storm of night thoughts.[31] But whether they were distortions or revelations of the physical world, the fears and fantasies evoked through night's long parenthesis were psychic realities, drawn out from that inner place, special to the Romantic poet, "where darkness makes abode, and all the host / Of shadowy things work endless changes."[32]

In "The Motive for Metaphor," similarly, the "shrinking" from primary noon seeks not only escape from the mysterious reality represented by the final X, but also revelation of that reality's less stable and less visible aspects: the "obscure world of things that could never be quite expressed." Most of life's great forces, "vital, arrogant, fatal, dominant," remain unmastered by systematic reason, not because they are supernatural but simply because things change, and because "Much less is known than not, / More far than near," as Philip Larkin says.[33] Normally, in problematic situations we have to proceed guided only by imaginative analogical extensions of beliefs more firmly held and sometimes more firmly based—which is to say, by metaphor. Occasionally, a fresh metaphor may give us a new hypothesis to try where routine fails. We fear the sound of "words without meaning" amid the dead leaves of autumn, but the Apollonian enlightenment of noon can never entirely clarify that darker "second part of life."

Metaphor, then may shrink from midday sunlight toward reality as well as away from it; and the curious syntax of the long four-stanza concluding sentence of "The Motive for Metaphor" allows the poem to offer both possibilities at once.

> In the same way, you were happy in spring,
>
> . . . . .
> Desiring the exhilarations of changes:
> The motive for metaphor, shrinking from
> The weight of primary noon,
> The A B C of being,
>
> The ruddy temper . . .
>
> . . . . .
> The vital, arrogant, fatal, dominant X.[34]

The final phrases, starting with "The A B C of being," seem at first to stand in apposition to "primary noon," so that the motive for metaphor is to shrink from the brutal reality designated by all of them, down through the final X. But as Patricia Parker has noted, sense and syntax also allow reading some or all of the concluding phrases in apposition to "the motive for metaphor," and hence in *opposition* to "the weight of primary noon." This gives the sense: "The motive for metaphor, shrinking from the [distracting] weight of primary noon, [is to reveal] the . . . X" of reality.[35] This antithetical reading accounts better than the primary one for certain paradoxical aspects of the conclusion—the strikingly metaphoric character of its images, their increasing obscurity, and the transitory character of their midday moments, glows, sparks, sounds, and flashes.[36]

This secondary obscure reading intertwines with the bright obvious one to make a chiaroscuro play on the ambiguity of the motive(s) for metaphor. What does the resulting ambiguity do for the poem's legal interpretation? The primary reading has "The Motive for Metaphor" warning of the dangers of lawyers' locating their subject too much in literature's obscure world of rustling leaves and melting clouds, too little in the harsh smithy of noonday sweat and violence. The secondary reading, the other side that Stevens brings us to hear after resisting our intelligence almost successfully, warns of an opposed jurisprudential danger.

The culturally oriented legal theorist notes, against the legal positivist stress on law as simply regularized coercion, that violence must be justified and legitimated by precept before it can be effective law; brute force cannot rule large populations without the support of ideology. The chancellor indeed has the force of the police behind him, but the police also have behind them the authority of the berobed chancellor, armed with his leather-bound books. The resulting pattern resists representation in a simple flow-chart; we are better served by an Escher drawing—or a Stevens poem.

Central to law's authority is its claim to operate impersonally, by exact and impartial reason, ideally expressed in transparent prose. Repeated critical exposure of the formalist myth that legal rules follow inexorably from its structure of concepts has failed to undermine law's central concepts themselves—contract, property, injury, obligation, rule. Like the Freudian repressed, these abstractions return to operate on legal judgment, not as the conceptual elements of axioms, but as powerful *metaphors.*

As metaphors they do not dictate judgment, but influence it partly by their very power of intimation, their evocation of the feelings and tacit associations that constitute the part of reality most resistant to straightforward representation in plain prose. The motive for metaphor, in this secondary legal version of the poem, is thus not the *evasion* of the law's hard realities, but rather the *revelation* of two of the most basic of those realities: the inability of law's language to encompass the world it would regulate; and the inescapable link between language and feeling in establishing the hold over opinion that distinguishes law from brute physical coercion.

Hobbes said that in government, clubs are trumps, whereas Hume said with equal certainty that opinion rules the world. Locke contrasted honest plain prose with deceptive figurative speech, whereas Nietzsche treated literal language as a crust of dead metaphor that masks living reality. "The Motive for Metaphor," read jurisprudentially in its full ambiguity, asserts both sides of both oppositions, insisting to believers in each thesis that "this is not all; hear the other side." In so doing, it does not simply engage in a self-canceling assertion of P and not-P. Like most practical principles, Hobbes's and Hume's political maxims, and Locke's and Nietzsche's theories of language, are not sharp-edged algorithms but heuristic guides, each modified by an implicit *sometimes.*

What does the lawyer gain by learning this from poetic intimation rather than prose statement? Here is one possible answer, to be tested against the reader's experience with "The Motive for Metaphor." The exercise of working through to both sides of the poem's antitheses, with the intelligence resisted and the feelings involved at each step, may better simulate, hence better teach,

65

the exercise of legal judgment in a live dispute than could following any set of arguments in analytic prose. (This may be so even if one of the lessons is restraint of emotional response.)

The exercise is useful as practice in the difficult art of holding antitheses in thought at the same time; the natural tendency is to treat Hobbes's and Hume's maxims, or Locke's and Nietzsche's, as logical contraries, and so to expel one of each from the mind, with bad practical results for a working theory of law-politics or of language. This is especially so for lawyers, who are taught that law is the application of logic to human affairs, and who dream of a transparent and complete legal code, a practical geometry of human affairs.

Against this temptation, lawyers may find it corrective to wrestle with a poem's antitheses and then to find that after the struggle has gone as far as it practically can, there remains the sense—which should likewise always hover over the reduction of a living dispute to a case at law—that not everything has been said, that representation in every respect has been partial and incomplete. Something of the same point can be made in favor of the standard pedagogic use of cases in law; we law professors use prose narrative (the statement of facts) rather than verse as a rhetorical means for inducing identification and suggesting incompletion, and hence for simulating the context of actual argument and judgment.

There are two differences, though, between the genres of case and poem. First, the facts of a case skillfully stated flow easily, "naturally"; poetry requires extra concentration in reading, and can thereby intensify and fuse both emotional and intellectual response. Second, a story well told can sound like the whole truth, though of course it never is.[37] Poetry, especially Stevens's kind of poetry, reminds the reader that the bright obvious is not everything; that something, which may be the most important thing, always remains obscure; that a principle, a moral of the story, always carries its own implicit qualification.

Consider in this light, finally, the most opaque of the metaphors in Stevens's poem, "steel against intimation." The phrase appears parenthetically among the four figures that suggest the blacksmith's forge:

> The ruddy temper, the hammer
> Of red and blue, the hard sound—
> Steel against intimation—the sharp flash,
> The vital, arrogant, fatal, dominant X.

The steel (hammer) is at home in the forge. But what, in a smithy, corresponds to "intimation"?

It is presumably the absence of any obvious answer that leads Helen Vendler to find in "steel against intimation" an executioner's blade against flesh, and then to call the succeeding sharp flash "surgical."[38] That reading fits with the primary jurisprudential interpretation of the poem, which locates law's powers to inflict pain and death in the hot place of high noon. Yet the reading leaves "steel against intimation" incongruous with an otherwise consistent (forge-related) set of surrounding phrases.[39]

Suppose, alternatively, that we drop the conventionally masculine assumption that dominant steel must overcome yielding intimation; imagine the steel not as the blacksmith's hammer, but as the metal to be worked.[40] This generates a second legal image to place alongside the executioner's blade cutting through flesh. In this one, the intimating and metaphorizing imagination heats and softens the steel of an impersonal rule of law, so that at the decisive moment of legal judgment the jurist can reshape the rule for the task at hand.

"Steel against intimation" then juxtaposes two aspects of law: its sharp rigidity, which maintains order and dominance, sometimes fatally; and its flexibility before the imagination, which maintains vitality but tempts its servants to arrogant self-assertion. These correspond to the two relations between poetry and law portrayed in the poem as a whole: they are separate spheres; they are intertwining webs.

V

A Change Not Quite Completed

> We seek
> Nothing beyond reality. Within it,
> Everything, the spirit's alchemicana
> Included . . .
>
> —Wallace Stevens,
> "An Ordinary Evening in New Haven"

> Does it move to and fro or is it of both
> At once? Is it a luminous flittering
> Or the concentration of a cloudy day?
>
> —Wallace Stevens,
> "Notes toward a Supreme Fiction"

If the poet Stevens speaks to lawyers, is it as a legal theorist? Probably not, according to the standard version of law and literature, which advertises itself as an interdisciplinary antidote to legal scholarship's recent turn toward theory.[1] Also probably not according to many of Stevens's best commentators, who find illusory his appearance of writing philosophically about reason-reality and imagination-unreality. And finally, Stevens himself said many times that he did not mean to philosophize or theorize, but only tried to be as pure a poet as he possibly could.

Against this weight of opinion, though, I want to say that he was not an antitheorist or counterphilosopher, but rather, as some recent commentators have suggested, a poetic *pragmatist* philosopher—the kind of theorist who constantly puts in question the status of theory itself and its relation to practice.[2] Pragmatism, as William James conceived it, was a philosophical mediation of "tough-minded" materialism and "tender-minded" idealism.[3] In jurisprudence, this means that pragmatism mediates between positivistic and instrumentalist conceptions of law on the one hand, and, on the other, idealist legal theories that identify law with the aspiration to justice, and see legal ideas as partly constitutive of social reality. Today this places the legal pragmatist between theories that analyze law mainly in terms of economics and rational-choice theory, and those that urge the legal centrality of disciplines that study values, ideology, language, and the interpretation of culture—the same division discussed in Chapter III.[4] There, I concluded that Stevens revealed in practice a positivist rather than culture-centered or mediated view of law, and that he kept law sharply segregated (Posner-style) from poetry in his own life.

If the poet Stevens had nothing direct to say about law, what can he bring more indirectly to lawyers by way of these legal-theoretic debates? As a start to answering this question, I will generalize from the previous chapter's discussion toward a more schematic account of his pervasive "reality-imagination complex," and then use the sketch to join the long-standing debate over whether Stevens is rightly regarded as a theoretical or philosophical poet, before concluding with a few remarks on what his version of theory or philosophy can say specifically to lawyers.

Stevens's poetic instrument plays variations on three basic movements of thought. First is the romantic or idealist quest to escape a dispirited and impoverished reality by enhancing and transcending it in imagination. Second is the realist movement back to bare ground, to the particular things themselves, purging thought and language of the imagination's cloudy clichés, its farfetched metaphors, its false integrations.[5] Third is the perspectivist reaction against the reality-imagination distinction itself, stressing that each version of reality is only a version, a fiction partly imagined; that perception and reason are themselves interpretive and imaginative processes; that literal speech is made of metaphors temporarily become commonplace; that mind and language are themselves part of reality; and that, in turn, even "natural" reality is in part socially constructed. The perspectivist movement can take either of two forms: a dialectical integration or synthesis of imagination and reality, "the concentration of a cloudy day"; or the acceptance of an unresolved dialogic oscillation between them, "a luminous flittering."

Let me now spell out this scheme in more detail, with particular reference to Stevens's treatment of the place of metaphor—that characteristic trope of romantic idealism—in poetry.[6] The romantic approach to metaphor is summarized by one of the previous chapter's epigraphs: "Reality is a cliché from which we escape by metaphor." The continuation of the adage identifies metaphor with poetry: "and it is only *au pays de la métaphore qu'on est poète*"—it is only in the land of metaphor that one is a poet.[7] The poet's imagination creates an alternative world that is imaginary or "unreal," a term that Stevens uses without pejorative connotations.[8] The need to escape from reality's "violence without" justifies the imagination's defensive "violence from within."[9] The "escape" of poetic idealism is no cowardly evasion but a heroic quest or an exile's return—the Exodus, the Odyssey, the purgatorial ascent, the pilgrimage, the search through memory for renovating spots of time, the revolutionary striving for justice. This is the theme at the heart of the greatest poetry, for "poetry . . . is essentially romantic."[10] In his romantic phase Stevens said that "metaphor has its aspect of the ideal,"[11] and sought supreme fictions, great metaphors that could refresh and hence transform a disenchanted modern world.

In his realist movement, Stevens turns against metaphor as a falsifying trope, an expression of the weak romantic; in this mood, he speaks of metaphor as "evasion" and proclaims the need to bypass it so as to reach bare reality, "the centre that I seek," as the second epigraph to the previous chapter has it.[12] The poet's "necessary angel" is "the angel of reality," in whose sight we escape our habituated blindness and "see the earth again, / Cleared of its stiff and stubborn, man-locked set."[13] Metaphors are "wormy," the false romantic is "rot," the "actual become anaemic."[14] It is in this phase that Stevens celebrates the clear wintry vision that confronts things as they are, free of the subjectivities of elation or gloom.[15]

70

In his third or perspectivist phase, Stevens questions the "reality-imagination" distinction altogether, and undermines all unqualified realist or idealist affirmations. Both epigraphs to the last chapter illustrate the process of qualification. "Reality is a cliché from which we escape by metaphor" is, on its face, an assertion of romantic idealism; metaphor leads us from a boring lifeless reality into the vital world of the imagined. But clichés are not always dull *truths*—sometimes they are falsehoods, unexamined conventional wisdom, part of "the stubborn, man-locked set" of built-up prejudice and error that hides from the mind the world as it really is. A good metaphor may reveal the truth by stripping away layers of habitual error; this is the uncovering use of imagination and metaphor promoted both by the high Romantics, and by those modern theories that tell the artist to "make it strange" so as to see things as they are. [16]

Now (to see Stevens's undermining at work in the opposite direction) consider the other, strongly realist and antimetaphoric, epigraph:

Trace the gold sun about the whitened sky
Without evasion by a single metaphor.
Look at it in its essential barrenness
And say this, this is the centre that I seek. [17]

On second thought, this realism leads away from reality: taken literally, the poet's command to look at the sun will produce blindness rather than discovery. [18] The lines quoted are preceded by the exorbitantly metaphoric command to "see it with the hottest fire of sight" and followed by "Fix it in an eternal foliage / And fill the foliage with arrested peace." Here, as so often, Stevens embeds his antifigurative realist vision in metaphor: ground cleared of metaphor by metaphoric fire blooms again with metaphoric vegetation.

Stevens deals explicitly (for him) with his perspectivist view of the imagination-reality distinction in his essay "Imagination as Value." [19] He begins by distinguishing between imagination as understood in aesthetics, the special creative fiction-making faculty of the artist, and "imagination as metaphysics," a term he borrows from Ernst Cassirer. Stevens first repudiates its philosophically idealist interpretation, and then uses it to refer to what we would call the social construction of reality—the fact that most of our ordinary concepts, including our frameworks for representing time and space, are imaginative and culturally specific constructs that well could have been otherwise. "Thou art not August unless I make thee so," Stevens puns.[20] This working of the imagination through everyday life is generally invisible to people within their own culture, for whom it forms their reality or "life-world." Its unveiling is left to the ethnographer (and the poet).

The whole essay, though somewhat difficult because of Stevens's allusive style, is an important exploration of topics central to contemporary thought. Stevens shows us that the boundary between the aesthetic and "life-world" uses of the imagination— the boundary between art and life—is unstable, since the whole social order of discursive "spheres" is itself an imaginative cultural construct "in continual flux."[21] Art and religion, he says—and I would add law—are "spheres" (current jargon would label them "systems"), all permeable to the pervasive environment of the life-world, and to each other.

I have spent the most space on Stevens's last or perspectivist movement precisely because it *is* so contemporary—an early version of those postmodernist critiques of foundational theories of knowledge and correspondence theories of truth now so popular among humanist intellectuals. The postmodernism of writers like Clifford Geertz and Richard Rorty (which has roots in Nietzsche and William James) strikes many today with the force of revelation; its converts often treat their former realist or idealist absolutisms as false creeds to be aggressively discarded. But such rooted world-views as idealism and realism are not transcended or purged easily; and postmodernists are often caught in the logical paradoxes of perspectivist self-reference ("there are no universal truths"), or—perhaps worse for paradox-loving humanists—the psychological and stylistic self-contradictions of perspectivist dogmatism and perspectivist cliché.

The move into perspectivism is typically dialectical in the Hegelian sense. The postmodernist begins with the critique of traditional idealism and realism as internally self-contradictory, and ascends to a synthesis where both thesis and antithesis are seen as merely partial and incomplete perspectives. Perspectivism, applied consistently to itself, would recognize this out-of-body vision of oneself peering through a biasing mental lens as only one situated (if perhaps temporarily privileged) perspective among many, not as a final resting place of thought. But taken as a philosophical theory, which claims to transcend while encompassing traditional realism and idealism, perspectivism can entrap its converts. Thus, Hegel, the thinker who saw the history of thought as an unceasing dialectical movement, announced that its end had arrived with himself and his system. It is not easy for the newly converted perspectivist to avoid this trap, to climb down from an *Aufhebung,* to go back to the farm after seeing Paree.

Stevens's poetry can serve as an antidote to the theorist's tendency to seek closure. Influenced, I believe, by William James's pluralist critique of the Hegelian absolute,[22] Stevens shows in his poetic practice a way to move on from the moment of dialectical synthesis or transcendence. Stevens sees the perspectival incompleteness of realism and idealism, but he also sees that even when these perspectives are recognized as limited, they will nevertheless survive the transcending moment of recognition. After the dialectical moment, dissolving (to take Stevens's example) the literal and metaphoric into one another, the idealist will reassert metaphor's vital superiority to lifeless literality, whereas the realist will again urge that the clarity of the literal should prevail against metaphoric evasion and obscurity. This happens because the perspectival differences are not entirely cognitive; rooted in temperament, habit, and mood, they are not easily argued away.

The difference between dialectic and dialogue, "concentration" and "luminous flittering," might be illustrated, psychologically, by the case of the young person who reads Jeremy Bentham and William Blake and is impressed by both—but is also perplexed because each so evidently rejects everything the other stands for.

Now suppose the young person reads Richard Rorty's effective postmodernist critique of both traditional realists and romantic idealists, and his resulting synthesis of the two approaches.[23] If convinced by the dialectical critique-cum-construction, the young person might expect to find in Rorty's sophisticated and illuminating but somewhat placid and world-weary formulation all that was best in Bentham and Blake—and hence might abandon them altogether.

This would be a mistake. An important synthesis presupposes a powerful thesis and antithesis; part of the power of the original terms is lost (though other value is gained) in the synthesis, however transcending. World-views take their character from what they exclude and emphasize as well as what they assert. With peculiar cogency, Bentham assaults (say) a New Age culture of cloudy nonsense in the name of reason and evidence, whereas Blake speaks for the human spirit and imagination against the universal dominance of a managerial and scientistic system of power. Each of these impassioned prophets turns a more intense light on certain aspects of experience than will ever be provided by more tolerant and catholic thinkers. When undivided attention to those aspects are what an individual or a society most needs, the exclusive realist or idealist will serve better than the inclusive perspectivist.

Implicit in this story, of course, is the ultimately perspectivist presumption that no single theory is ever likely to serve satisfactorily as an all-purpose guide to life. In Stevens's words, "The squirming facts exceed the squamous mind, / If one may say so."[24] From the story, there also follows a paradox: the perspectivist sometimes needs an intensity of focus that is most readily supplied by one variety or another of absolutism. Yet how can an absolutist view of the world continue to serve this focusing and intensifying function once it has been recognized as a partial perspective?

Stevens certainly holds the ultimately perspectivist premise, as do many contemporary theorists; but his special contribution is a poetic practice that exemplifies a way to live with, and through, the practical paradox of perspectivism. He illustrates both the paradox and the escape in the last six cantos of his most important philosophical poem, "Notes toward a Supreme Fiction." In the first of these cantos, Stevens's representative modern thinker, the broad- and high-minded Canon Aspirin, enjoys a meal of Meursault and lobster, and notes the satisfactions of his widowed sister's unimaginative but devoted life with her children. But the Canon's spiritual side is not satisfied, and while the family sleeps he meditates, and achieves a spiritual ascent to a mystical vision of a Dantesque point of light. The choice posed by the vision, as he sees it, is not "a choice between, but of"; he then opts for "the whole, / The complicate, the amassing harmony."

The good Canon, close as he is to Stevens in many ways, is an object of affectionate irony in the poem, though "the complicate, the amassing harmony" is sometimes quoted as the poet's own ideal.[25] But Stevens does not accept the Canon's project—lobster, kids, divine vision, the works—any more than he accepts other formulations of a static, all-encompassing synthesis. Stevens was more obviously ironic in an earlier portrayal of dialectical resolution:

> The imagined and the real, thought
> And the truth, Dichtung und Wahrheit, all
> Confusion solved.[26]

Here he is more subtle, but the point is the same. In the next canto the Canon, after his meditative ascent and consequent choice of "the whole," becomes dissatisfied with his attempt to erect objects of worship from his syncretic "complicate." He yearns, like Stevens's poetic alter ego Canon Eliot, for a sterner external discipline, something to rescue him from the enslaving freedom of inclination, improvisation, and ennui; he is desperate "to discover an order . . . to find, / Not to impose . . . It is possible, possible, possible. It must / Be possible." He aspires to an objectively certified amassing complicate, but no such thing (in Stevens's pragmatist-perspectivist world) is to be had.[27]

In the poem's final three cantos, Stevens dismisses the Canon in order to speak in his own voice. Here as elsewhere in his poetry, he insists that, in the absence of a single world-theory or transcendent vision, we must reduce our demands. He will play the whole harmonium; romance, realism, and perspectivism itself (as a temporary perspective)—each has its moment, and its canto. Only in such a seasonlike cycle does Stevens believe that "major weather"—the full range of humanly accessible reality—can be found. Each stage involves exclusions, imperfections, incompletions; no "whole" or "amassing harmony" can ever be present to experience at once. The idealist rejects (and romantically disdains) the quotidian reality of repetition, daily work, domesticity; the realist rejects (and bluntly scorns) the romantic quest for the sublime; the perspectivist rejects (and ironically patronizes) the narrow though more intense focus of these two less encompassing views.

A practical question for the convinced perspectivist is how, after the moment of transcendence in which realism and romance are seen only as perspectives, to regain the intensity, passion, and commitment that each carries with it when accepted as an absolute conception of the world. Here Stevens's solution (expressed in a prose epigram) is a pragmatic one, with roots in the Romantic poets, Nietzsche, and William James: "The final belief is to believe in a fiction, which you know to be a fiction, there being nothing else. The exquisite truth is to know that it is a fiction and that you believe in it willingly." [28] When faced with the challenge that to believe in a fiction was a psychologically impossible trick, Stevens replied that we all do it every day, in literature and life. Literature requires a "willing suspension of disbelief," life a "will to believe" beyond what is justified by evidence and logic. [29] We can enjoy literature; we manage to live life; therefore, we can believe (using the pragmatic sense of "belief") in fictions. [30] "Fiction" is a crucially multivocal term for Stevens; it connotes falsity to the realist, the heightened reality of creative invention to the idealist, and "madeness" or social construction to the perspectivist.

Stevens's reinstatement of the dialogue of realism and idealism

76

after the moment of perspectivist insight is well illustrated in "An Ordinary Evening in New Haven." The whole long poem is an experiment in how far poetry can pursue the reductive realist spirit: the poet begins with "the eye's plain version" and keeps "coming back and coming back / To the real," but is invariably reminded that reality includes as one of its plain facts the workings of the imagination, "the spirit's alchemicana."[31]

Mooning on this oscillation can turn us into dialectical metaphysicians who imagine as our static final truth an absolute substratum in which

> The enigmatical
> Beauty of each beautiful enigma
> Becomes amassed in a total double-thing.

But to come to rest in this amassing harmony would be to join the bronze man in the moon, "whose mind was made up and who, therefore, died." We escape imaginative extinction by getting on with it: "allons." The rattle of the milkman's bottles breaks the moonlit stillness, and soon the sun will rise to "make gay the hallucinations in surfaces."[32]

Stevens does not regard the dualism of matter and mind, reality and imagination, as some easily discarded bit of philosophical entrepreneurship. He imagines it arising on the first day, when part of the self "held fast tenaciously in common earth," and part looked to the moonlit sky for "such majesty as it could find." The first self, Alpha, morning's reality-seeker, sets out alone and naked, cherishing the freshness of beginnings, while Omega, the evening's hierophant of the imagination, magnificently robed, holds court among "luminous vassals" that are like clouds around the moon. The two achieve no meeting of minds; both consider themselves the "custodians of the glory of the scene" and "immaculate interpreters of life." The "difference" between cat and rabbit remains: "Alpha continues to begin. / Omega is refreshed at every end."[33]

We must remember that Stevens's ironies at the expense of too easy synthesis—the Canon's "amassing harmony," the "total double-thing," the "all confusion solved"[34]—do not signal a total rejection of the possibilities of synthesis, "the concentration of a cloudy day." The possibility of imaginative (metaphoric) integration remained at the heart both of his secular religion and his account of daily life. In his poetry, he sought to experience and capture those moments, "accessible to . . . the acutest poet," when "what is real and what is imagined are one"; in them the poet could "forget need's golden hand" and find "that occasional ecstasy, or ecstatic freedom of the mind, which is his special privilege"—and which his readers are privileged, in some measure, to share.[35] There are the little integrations, as when a Gauguinesque planter who fled from the cold north to a tropical island dies "sighing that he should leave the banjo's twang";[36] and the large ones, as when, in Stevens's best-known lines, a few details of a landscape serve to integrate a closing frontier, a cooling universe, and a dying God.* Every Stevens reader has a private anthology of such moments; they are what first drew us to him.

Further, as we have seen, Stevens recognized that as imaginative integrations cross from art into the life-world and join common speech and thought, they gradually harden and attach themselves to the reeflike structure of collective thought. For Stevens, every religion exemplifies this process, as do "the four seasons and the twelve months." But while imagination integrates wholes that exceed the sum of their parts in both art and life, there is no method, no logic, that guarantees these integrations. The world remains distributed largely into its separate parts, elements whose relations with each other, if happy at all, are contrapuntal and dialogic rather than harmonious and synthetic.

---

*Deer walk upon our mountains, and the quail
  Whistle about us their spontaneous cries;
  Sweet berries ripen in the wilderness;
  And, in the isolation of the sky,
  At evening, casual flocks of pigeons make
  Ambiguous undulations as they sink
  Downward to darkness, on extended wings.

  ("Sunday Morning," viii, *CP,* 70)

To summarize, Stevens moves from idealism to realism, then dialectically to an integrating perspectivism, then back out (or down) to a renewed dialogic oscillation of idealism and realism—now with the dialogue partners reconceived as perspectives. The freedom with which he moves is indeed exhilarating; but what should we make of a "thinker" with so casual an attitude toward consistency? "One often says contradictory things,"[37] he wrote in a letter to a young admirer, and he certainly seemed to: Hobbes was right to say that force rules, but so was Hume when he mentioned that opinion does; the world exists entirely in the mind, but we are biological mechanisms; "imagination is the only genius," but "we have to accept reality itself as the only genius."[38]

Acute readers of Stevens often follow the course Denis Donoghue describes, from the belief that Stevens is "chiefly a philosophic poet," plumbing epistemological issues, to the conclusion that "knowledge is only the interest of a mood among many moods . . . I would now read Stevens's ostensibly philosophic poems as poems of pleasure; exalted pleasure, indeed, as when a mind circulates among its possibilities."[39]

In his letters and lectures, Stevens himself seems to confirm this latter description. "I am not a philosopher," he says in no uncertain terms.[40] He took up philosophic constructs "as tentative ideas for the purposes of poetry"; he read philosophy "as a substitute for fiction"; and he would be "bored to death at the mere thought" of systematically studying it.[41] He had "no wish to arrive at a conclusion" on the central issue of imagination versus reality, but rather, as Donoghue suspected, followed his moods: "Sometimes I believe in the imagination for a long time and then, without reasoning about it, turn to reality and believe in that and that alone."[42]

But while this all seems an unqualified rejection of any philosophic claims on Stevens's part, such a thing rarely occurs in his work: he always has an ear and a word for the other side. He *was* a philosopher in one sense, and knew it, just as in another sense he knew that he was not. When a commentator concluded that Stevens got "nowhere in particular" in his poetic play with reality

and the imagination, the poet objected: "I do at least arrive at the
end of my logic. And where that leaves me ought to be perfectly
clear to you." It was true that "we are dealing with poetry, not
with philosophy," but what he meant by that was that he did not
want to "formulate a system."[43]

Stevens was indeed not a systematic philosopher; he had no
interest in elaborating his version of the Truth, an overall conceptual scheme covering all or some large region of reality. Of course,
many distinguished contemporary philosophers likewise have no
system-building ambitions. Second, Stevens did not *argue* toward
conclusions; he proceeded by association or intimation from insight to insight rather than by inference from premise or evidence
to conclusion. But in this he followed the tradition of such philosophical aphorists as the preacher of *Ecclesiastes,* Montaigne,
Emerson, Pascal; and such aphoristic philosophers as the Greek
pre-Socratics, Bacon, Nietzsche, and the later Wittgenstein. A
reigning (though decreasingly firm) consensus among Anglo-
American academic philosophers excludes nonargumentative
writing of this kind from philosophy; without debating the juris-
dictional point, let us agree at least to call these figures thinkers.

They *are* thinkers (and philosophers to those with a more catholic view of the subject) because in some sense, however playfully
or ironically, they affirm what they say. The question is whether
Stevens the poet affirms anything, or rather evades all but aesthetic judgment with the dramatist's defense that he is merely
portraying. Yet if he had meant only to circulate playfully among
his possibilities, why did he resent a critics saying that he did not
get anywhere? "I affirm," he began the last couplet of one of his
philosophical poems; but as always there was a qualification: "and
then at midnight the great cat / Leaps quickly from the fireside
and is gone."[44]

Does this form of qualification, in which the thinker explicitly
labels his affirmations temporary and fleeting, brand him a spiritual drifter or an intellectual chameleon? What should we finally
make of that side of Stevens that (in "The Motive for Metaphor")

inhabited "an obscure world / In which you were never quite yourself / And did not want nor have to be?" Drawing an acceptable line between creative adaptivity on the one hand, and weakness or failure of identity on the other, was from his earliest youth an important issue to the poet.[45] As he grew older, he came more and more explicitly to terms with his need to maintain his negative capability, his access to that androgynous state of "vague receptivity" in which he felt like "one part of something that is dependent on another part, which he is not quite able to specify."[46] At his best, he saw this not as evasion or irresponsibility but as personal and artistic integrity.[47]

At the same time, he was never entirely confident in his faith; in his less secure moments, Stevens feared the judgment of the philosophers, the stern male followers of Descartes and Locke, to whom circulation among possibilities and "vague receptivity" was not compatible with the manly and intellectually responsible pursuit of truth. Stevens submitted his essay "Collect of Philosophy" to a professional philosophy journal, and was disappointed though not surprised when it was rejected.[48] Stevens well knew the other language, the tight prose he had criticized Roger Caillois for failing to achieve. His legal letters and memoranda were not dialogic celebrations of the possibilities of play and paradox. We must recall his sharp separation of law and philosophy, grouped together under the heading "reason," from the rabbit's after-hours world of poetry and imagination.[49]

But as I noted when discussing this separation in Chapter III, the starkness of the opposition has to be qualified when we look more carefully at the contrasts Stevens drew between poetry and philosophy. One such contrast emerges when we compare his anticipatory elegy to the systematic philosopher George Santayana with the valedictory he wrote when he had finally collected his own life's work. Santayana, the philosopher, dying in a convent in Rome, in a simple room with only "a bed, a chair, and moving nuns," comes to "the immensest theatre, the pillared porch" of his philosophic system:

> Total grandeur of a total edifice,
> Chosen by an inquisitor of structures
> For himself. He stops upon this threshold,
> As if the design of all his words takes form
> And frame from thinking and is realized.[50]

"Realized," as always in Stevens, is an honorific term, carrying the double sense of "apprehended" and "made real"; this passage thus celebrates the high human achievement of creating a new reality by imaginatively reworking things as they are.[51]

But when Stevens came to accept and celebrate the closure of his own life's work, he chose different imagery. His collected poems made up "the planet on the table"—not a cathedral or temple, but a microcosm of the green and fluent mundo, revolving around the sun of his imagination, its poems thus "makings of the sun," like plants, though he hoped longer-lived. His ultimate wish for these poems was not that they should be able to stand by themselves, final in their grandeur, like a philosopher's system, but that they should bear

> Some lineament or character,
> Some affluence, if only half-perceived,
> In the poverty of their words,
> Of the planet of which they were part.[52]

We have here the traditional romantic contrast between the vital-organic and the artificial-geometric: "The earth is not a building but a body," as Stevens once put it.[53] Still, it is important to see that his portrayal of the philosopher's way is anything but hostile; Santayana's temple is a noble edifice, clear in line and free from obscurity, an achievement to take pride in—even if not quite a world.[54]

Other comparisons Stevens made between poetry and philosophy fill out the picture of the contrast as he saw it. In his essay "The Figure of the Youth as a Virile Poet,"[55] he said that philosophers and poets pursue different forms of truth—logical truth and empirical truth, respectively. Whereas people read philosophy for logical possibility, they read poetry, he said, for fact: not "bare fact," but "fact beyond their perception in the first instance and outside the normal range of their sensibility."[56] Elsewhere, he specified poets' special descriptive domain as the inner life.[57] The Stevensian poet is a phenomenologist—just as are philosophers and psychologists such as Husserl and Heidegger (whom he had not read), and William James (whom he had).

The reference to James leads to a final comparison, one Stevens made in his essay "Collect of Philosophy." Poets and philosophers, he says, are united in their devotion to "probing for an integration" of experience, but they differ in their ends: "The philosopher intends his integration to be fateful; the poet intends his to be *effective*."[58] The poet's theorizing, then, is to be judged not on the basis of its final and comprehensive truth, but rather by the pragmatic test, which Stevens often in fact applied to his own formulations.[59]

Of course, some (few) philosophers, most notably William James, have explicitly applied the same test to their own efforts, and Stevens as a poetic thinker is not only a pragmatist, but closer to James than to any other philosopher. There are many parallels: both used the pragmatic test—Stevens thought poetry should "help people lead their lives," as James believed philosophy should do; both had a pluralistic bias against the dialectical Absolute; both were strong naturalists, who were also troubled by nostalgia for a traditional god; both endorsed the "will to believe" in fictions that could infuse life with morale and meaning; and finally, both held the view James called "radical empiricism," the belief in experience as a category that precedes the division between subject and object, self and nature.[60]

Almost uniquely among philosophers, James argued that philosophical disputes were the intellectual formulations of temperamental differences, which was why they could not be settled by reason alone.[61] Stevens described "poetic truth" as "agreement with reality," hence *fact;* but fact found by the imagination of an imaginative person and "expressed in terms of his personality."[62] This account "appears" to make "final" the difference between poetic and philosophic truth, he says ironically—because philosophers (with few exceptions beyond James) claim final and impersonal truth for their formulations.

If we accept the pragmatic test of thought, and pragmatism's stress on thought as a manifestation of the whole personality—emotion and intellect together—the distinction between merely poetically playing with ideas and philosophically affirming them is considerably blurred. Where correspondence tests of belief seem particularly hard to apply (in areas of theory, morality, and religion), pragmatist conceptions are most plausible; we entertain ideas as fictions or hypotheses, or provisionally adopt them as beliefs, because they help us get through the world in some way other than by accurately depicting it. They are, in Stevens's words, descriptions without place.

For example, Stevens answers the essentially religious question "What am I to believe?" with a deliberate *fiction,* derived imaginatively from the sunset, of an angel that leaps down through space; he then poses the return question: "Am I that imagine this angel less satisfied" because the angel is fictive?[63] The question is not rhetorical; Stevens is writing "notes toward" an overarching account of life. He expects that the reader's answers will emerge as a total personality tries to live with and through the fiction. If we add to the notion of personality as a defined "substance that prevails" the further inevitability of fluctuating moods, *allegro* and *penseroso,* the notion that apparently contradictory statements may pragmatically serve the same person at different times becomes yet easier to understand and accept.[64]

Sometimes it is right to hold in mind that the early bird catches the worm; sometimes, that all work and no play make Jack a dull boy. Hobbes's maxim that in politics clubs are trumps and Hume's that opinion rules the world stand in a similar relation, as do principles proclaiming the centrality of rules and of equitable discretion in legal judgment. To say this kind of thing (as James and Stevens so readily do) is not to embrace unreason or deny the Law of Contradiction. General propositions of some use in the world, outside the most exact of the sciences, are almost always probabilistic or defeasible in form rather than universal

and axiomatic; their implicit logical operator is not "for all x,"
but "for some x" (or "for all x, unless . . . " with the defeating
conditions not fully specified). This does not render them useless
or even dispensable, but in cases where general beliefs conflict, it
leaves the decision to judgment (or "perception," as Aristotle put
it) rather than to computation.[65]

For lawyers, whose business is the formulation and application
of generalizations meant to cover particular cases, no truth is
more important, or more difficult. The main problem does not
arise from disagreement with the proposition that judgment is
inescapable in law, but from a more potent and less intellectual
source: the inveterate (and no doubt survival-adaptive) "longing
after certainty and repose that is in every human mind."[66] Stevens's utility for lawyers, that peculiarly hungry segment of cer-
tainty-starved humanity, is his almost preternatural ability to
represent the workings of the spirit's alchemicana through all its
phases: the bright sun, the obscure moon, the moments of con-
centrated cloud and of luminous flittering.[67] To experience so
vivid a portrayal of this inner process of assertion, qualification,
and qualified reassertion is to come closer to grasping that, as
Holmes put it, "certainty generally is illusion and repose is not
the destiny of man," or, in Stevens's words: "It can never be satisfied, the mind, never."[68]

VI

The Colors of the Mind

Inescapable romance, inescapable choice
Of dreams, disillusion as the last illusion . . .

—Wallace Stevens,
"An Ordinary Evening in New Haven"

I've brought you here through intellect and skill;
from now on let pleasure be your guide . . .

—Dante, *Purgatorio*, XXVII

When Stevens came to write his most comprehensive poem, "Notes toward a Supreme Fiction," he organized it around three central imperatives. First, a supreme fiction or life-theory must be revelatory, must have what truth a fiction can have ("It Must Be Abstract").[1] Second, it must help, cure, transform, make a difference to, its audience ("It Must Change"—I read the verb as primarily transitive). Finally, because Stevens's conception is of a *poem* (or myth, or story) striving to be a theory, "It Must Give Pleasure." Not by chance, these divisions roughly match mine of the previous chapter, where I divided Stevens's thought into tendencies toward realism, romanticism, and perspectivism. They also roughly correspond to the three canticles of the *Divine Comedy,* which it was Stevens's immense ambition to rewrite for those who "live in the world of Darwin and not the world of Plato."[2]

In the last chapter, we saw how Stevens might speak to lawyers (those with ears to hear) about a familiar topic of legal theory—the opposition and interplay of permanent reasoned truth ("abstraction") and imaginative transformation ("change"). Now we come to the less familiar issue of the place of *pleasure* in the legal theorist's work. Lawyers know about Hell and Purgatory; but what have they to do with Heaven?

According to a standard legal-theoretic story, Strict Law is conceived as reason's check on pleasure's unruly promptings—an essential check for populace and rulers alike. First, anarchy unleashes the insatiable pursuit of individual pleasure, and the resulting war of all against all makes life solitary, poor, nasty, brutish, and short. Supplanting anarchy with Leviathan, the absolute government of men, allows bare survival, but leaves the populace at the pleasure of power-corrupted tyrants. The next step, aimed at achieving maximum collective pleasure through limitation on both the anarchic and tyrannical operations of the pleasure principle, is the Rule of Strict Law. Here, rulers and citizens alike operate under definite rules, clear commands that can be understood and applied by all, subject to ultimate enforcement only through independent judges whose primary allegiance is not to any regime or faction but to the law itself.

According to the Rule of Strict Law, all who can reason must be able to agree on what the law requires; legal judgment must thus be formal and deductive. Yet the deductive conception collides with another central moral of the stock legal story: the welfare of the people is the supreme law. When strict application of law's rules defeats its purposes, Equity is invoked to correct Strict Law, or (the same thing) law's spirit to correct its letter. The ever-present possibility of equitable correction converts all legal principles and rules from inflexible axioms into heuristic precepts whose shortfalls, overlaps, and conflicts must be resolved by judgment (Aristotle's "perception"). Yet because no sharp criterion distinguishes such exercise of discretionary judgment from decision by whim or pleasure, Equity carries within it the seeds of tyranny, if not of anarchy, and renews the case for Strict Law. Thus goes the familiar oscillation of strict and equitable legal theories, a pendulum swing punctuated by the occasional ambitious attempts to transcend or obliterate the very distinction between Strict Law and Equity.

Pleasure appears in this theoretical fable as the Other of Strict

Law, its (purely external) end or purpose, but at the same time its constant adversary in actual operation. Unrestricted private pursuit of pleasure is anarchy; government "at the pleasure" of rulers is tyranny. By contrast, Equity's chancellor indulges the pleasures of intuition, feeling, and empathy, the morality of the heart, in mitigation of the harsh rationalist rigor of rule-bound deductive legalism.

The standard story's assignment of pleasure to the side of Equity allows Strict Law an important advantage in the continuing debate, for in any dispute it casts doubt on the motives of Equity's champions. They are bending Strict Law for the sake of pleasure—their *own* pleasure, that is, the pleasures of the heart satisfied (or its empathic pains averted) by the intuitively fitting or responsive judgment, as against the harsh, unfeeling dictate of Strict Law. The legalists serve the *public* pleasure, the greatest happiness of the greatest number, by enforcing the Rule of Strict Law, and thereby ascetically denying themselves the private pleasures of response to the heart's (intuition's, judgment's) siren call.

The legalists' advantage here is the same one that John Locke claimed in his advocacy of plain dry prose instead of poetry and rhetoric in the conduct of the world's serious intellectual business. That business is inquiry into (as law is the practical administration of) "things as they are." To discern what *is,* Strict Law confines itself to the plain prose of juristic science, the language appropriate for use in the deductive application of a rational code. But Equity, in admitting discretionary judgment, allows itself indulgence in the pleasures of rhetoric, as the arts of story and metaphor move the judge's heart (intuition, judgment, perception) against the application of Strict Law in the particular case. Not by chance, Locke the political philosopher is as much the champion of the Rule of Strict Law as Locke the philosopher of science is the champion of the plain style.

Since the time of the Romantics, poets have tended to accept the dualistic Lockean framing of the issue: pleasure against reason, the heart against the head. Descartes and Newton join with Locke to make a composite enemy, supplemented by later positivists, of whom Bentham is the type. The scientists and their philosophers are said to have impoverished the world by banishing warmth and color in the name of cold impersonal truth, and to have forsaken the essential human heart or soul for the rule of that false god, that mere computer, the mind.

Present-day humanists, many still quivering from school-induced fear of mathematics, others resentful of the prestige and power of scientists in academe and beyond, are always tempted to accept this dualistic framing of the issue. Legal humanists too, in their recent revival, have tended to accept the stereotyped oppositions: Equity versus Strict Law: colored particularity versus colorless abstraction: rich complexity (irregular curves) versus reductive simplification (artificial straight lines); life versus mechanism; pleasure and spontaneity versus order and authority; and, perhaps the two master oppositions, warm versus cold and heart versus head. The obvious contemporary enemies are law and economics and other varieties of legal formalism. In addition, some feminist and third-world critics have mapped standard gender and race stereotypes onto these old oppositions, identifying women (versus men) as warmly nurturing, people of color (versus whites) as warmly soulful.

This allows some satisfying name-calling: the statisticians, economists, engineers, white males, whoever, are soulless, heartless, unimaginative, reductive, anal, dry, cold, whatever.[3] But I think joining issue on the terms set by these stock dualisms is in every way a mistake. Strategically, to accept the separation of heart and head and align with the heart in the ensuing party struggle is to relegate oneself to marginal, weekend, after-hours status—and to losing.

More substantively, the standard stereotyped dichotomies present a grotesquely impoverished picture of the life of the spirit, neglecting both the imagination, passion, and spontaneity involved in science and mathematics, and the hard thought, critical detachment, and pursuit of order involved in the writing and understanding of poetry. When the oppositions are transferred to law, the disaster should be clear; any theory that denies the essential place of rules, of order, and of reason in law neither can nor should have any hope of significant success.

An alternative approach is to show that truth-seeking and pleasure-seeking are so blended in both science and poetry as to be in practical terms inseparable. The title of an essay by William James supplies the essential slogan here: "The Sentiment of Rationality."[4] The strategy is to start by showing just how much sensation, emotion, and pleasure is bound up in the pursuit of cold reason and the pure order of the intellect.

It is in aid of this strategy that I finally return to Wallace Stevens, who in my view is one of its master exponents. This poet was "too cold" and made the most of it; he *felt* the "blessed rage for order"; as a young lawyer, he wrote in his journal: "It would be much *nicer* to have things definite . . . I think I'd enjoy being an executioner, or a Russian policeman."[5]

Let us listen to Stevens the poetic exponent of the feelings and pleasures that motivate the cause of Strict Law, the aesthetic of the cold Russian policeman. For initial contrast to this side of his work, take Keats's famous outcry against intellectual law and order, in the form of Newton's laws of optics:

> Philosophy will clip an Angel's wings,
> Conquer all mysteries by rule and line,
> Empty the haunted air and gnomed mine—
> Unweave a rainbow . . . [6]

In his early poem "Stars at Tallapoosa," Stevens confronts those cold geometric lines that for Keats "conquer[ed] all mysteries" and disenchanted the world. Stevens finds in them—"straight and swift between the stars"—their own enchantment. The starlines are "much too dark and much too sharp," he says, to be born of the night itself; rather, they are creations of the human mind, which through them "attains simplicity"—simplicity "by rule and line," in Keats's terms. Stevens contrasts their precision to the attractions they lack: lyricism and vitality ("moon . . . on silvered leaf," "melon-flower nor dew") and terrestrial richness and complexity ("sea-lines, moist" and "earth-lines, long and lax").

But nevertheless the star-lines are beautiful and pleasure-giving: "Let these be your delight, secretive hunter / . . . These lines are swift and fall without diverging." Nothing in nature

> Is like to these. But in yourself is like:
> A sheaf of brilliant arrows flying straight,
> Flying and falling straightway for their pleasure,
> Their pleasure that is all bright-edged and cold.

Finally, the joys of geometric thought resemble more usual and sensual pleasures:

> Or if not arrows, then the nimblest motions,
> Making recoveries of young nakedness
> And the lost vehemence the midnights hold.[7]

Thus geometric lust, the hot pursuit of cold beauty—as Stevens wrote elsewhere: "it is a singular romance / This warmth in the blood-world for the pure idea."[8]

Yvor Winters, in his influential critical attack on Stevens's "hedonism," condemns the "Tallapoosa" poem for what he calls its "absolute severance of the intellectual and the emotional." Stevens presents, so Winters says, the straight sky-lines of intellect and the irregular earth-lines of experience as "disparate and unrelated to one another; and *it follows, although this is not stated in the poem,* that the intellectual experience, since it bears no relationship to the rest of our life and hence is in no way useful, is valuable *simply* for the independent emotional satisfaction which one may derive from it."[9]

But here the rationalist critic projects a non sequitur; what Stevens does not state does not follow. The fact that pure reasoning "gives pleasure" does not detract from its practical importance. The "pleasure . . . bright-edged and cold" that Descartes, Newton, and Leibniz found in inventing analytic geometry and calculus undermines neither the truth nor the utility of their achievements. Probably some share of that pleasure has motivated every student who has since grasped these powerful instruments.

What Stevens's poem does emphasize is that thought has pleasures independent of utility. To invent or learn a logical paradox or a theorem of number theory that has no use whatever can bring bright-edged satisfaction. The lawyer grasping (or inventing) a "nice point of law" feels a similar pleasure, and this pleasure plays no small part in the continued importance of formalism and conceptualism in legal thought, in the face of a reasoned critique that has been sustained against them for generations.

The aesthetic of the "bright-edged and cold" also helps make an intellectually invalid but emotionally compelling association between ingenious formal reasoning and empirically accurate perception. Both deduction and clear vision are naturally *felt* as cold, linear, satisfying in their impersonality. But truly, as William James recognized when he placed the two tendencies on opposite sides of his antinomy between tough- and tender-mindedness, empiricist reliance on the evidence of the senses tends to reveal the world's inexhaustible and inexplicable plurality, and hence conflicts with the "tender" rationalist tendency to accept as real only experience that can be reduced to terms of elegant parsimony and simplicity.[10] Holmes's famous opposition between "logic" and "experience" in legal theory makes the same point—a point concealed by the conflating aesthetic of cold reduction.

"The Snow Man" shows the affective link, celebrating accurate perception with imagery that also evokes the geometric pleasures of the star-lines. We "must have a mind of winter" to look at a winter landscape while hearing no pathos or "misery" in the sound of the wind; to attain this state of objectivity is to achieve the gloriously transparent vision of one "who listens in the snow, / And, nothing himself, beholds / Nothing that is not there and the nothing that is." There, along with "the nothing," are earth's pleasures to the eye, not moist sea-lines or melon flowers, but quite as good in their clear and bright-edged way:

> . . . the junipers shagged with ice,
> The spruces rough in the distant glitter
> Of the January sun . . .[11]

In a later poem, Stevens strips this reductive epiphany of its perceptual content and intellectualizes it; the imagery and the appeal remain closely similar. The detritus of memory is banished and

> . . . the air is clear of everything.
> It has no knowledge except of nothingness
> And it flows over us without meanings,
> As if none of us had ever been here before
> And are not now.[12]

This is the joy of self-abnegating *impersonality,* in its feeling very much like the pleasures of an astronomer who contemplates a universe sublimely impersonal, vast, ancient, and indifferent to human strivings. To a certain temperament, which Stevens well understood, this is an inspiring vision, through which "we are loosened from the chains of a most narrow dungeon, and set at liberty to rove in a more august empire."[13] Submission both to the mind's logical operations and to the evidence of the senses brings the freedom and sense of mastery associated with the Enlightenment.

The scientist's self-effacing and open-eyed scrutiny gives a vision not only clearer but (again, by imagistic association rather than rational analogy) higher and more encompassing; it is the mountain climber's vision from the chilly heights, theoretical in the word's root sense of long-sighted. Thus, in "How to Live, What to Do," Stevens's favorite poem from his second volume, *Ideas of Order,* two climbers rested before their night assault on the "heroic height" of a rock. "Coldly the wind fell upon them," with a "sound / Joyous and jubilant and sure," as they prepared to ascend. With no help from "chorister, nor priest," these independent aristocrats of the spirit were now ready to climb "away from the muck of the land / That they had left."[14] The same Nietzschean association between cold, clarity of vision, and the courage to leave the herd is renewed in a much later poem, where the "refreshment of cold air, cold breath" and its accompanying "clearness" give birth to "a perfection emerging from a new known, / An understanding beyond journalism."[15] So the legal formalist Christopher Columbus Langdell promises mastery of

the "ever-tangled skein of human affairs," the muck of mere politics, through a long-sighted understanding that accurately identifies the fundamental principles that constitute "law, considered
as a science."[16]

The straight lines between the stars at Tallapoosa suggest as
well the pleasures of *repose* and *order.* Geometric truth (precisely
because it is a purely formal invention of the human imagination)
is eternal and unchanging, a symbolic defense against decay and
death. In "This Solitude of Cataracts," the poet wishes to put a
stop to the Heraclitean stream of experience which "kept flowing
and never the same way twice"; if he could put "his mind to rest"
in the "permanent realization" of a Platonic heaven of concepts,
he might be "released from destruction," a "bronze man" free
from the decay of mutable flesh, at "the azury centre of time."[17]
And again, in "Credences of Summer," he connects the Holmesian
legal formalist's "longing for certainty and repose" to the concept
of truth certain and unchanging, the Russian policeman's truth
seen in its most attractive light:

> The rock cannot be broken. It is the truth.
> . . . . .
> It is the visible rock, the audible,
> The brilliant mercy of a sure repose,
> On this present ground, the vividest repose,
> Things certain sustaining us in certainty.[18]

In "The Idea of Order at Key West" the ordering impulse
evokes from Stevens some of his strongest poetry, as he celebrates
the need to impose form, however arbitrary, on the otherwise incomprehensible chaos of the natural world. The beach-striding
singer's song took her "beyond the genius of the sea," since

> . . . what she sang was uttered word by word.
> It may be that in all her phrases stirred
> The grinding water and the gasping wind;
> But it was she and not the sea we heard.

For she was the maker of the song she sang.
The ever-hooded, tragic-gestured sea
Was merely a place by which she walked to sing.

When the listening poet and his companion turned back toward town, they connected the song's verbal ordering of the sea with the geometric lines made by the lights of the fishing boats, which, like the imagined lines ("ghostlier demarcations") of zodiac and latitude-longitude,

> Mastered the night and portioned out the sea
> Fixing emblazoned zones and fiery poles,
> Arranging, deepening, enchanting night
>
> Oh! Blessed rage for order, pale Ramon
> The maker's rage to order words of the sea
> Words of the fragrant portals, dimly-starred
> And of ourselves and of our origins,
> In ghostlier demarcations, keener sounds.[19]

Here "the sentiment of rationality" is no ascetic self-denial of pleasure, but a moment of grateful relief at the imposition of a fragment of order on otherwise uncontainable chaos.[20] A judge or legal theorist can be moved by the same "rage for order" to want to impose, policeman style, a sharp-edged code of positive law on a turbulent sea of otherwise unintelligible social life. Nor does the legal point run only one way politically: the oppressed may seek clear rules rather than vague standards as protection against social violence and official prejudice.

The final formalist's pleasure for our catalogue is the satisfaction associated with closure and perfection, which in the realm of thought is the satisfaction of creating or possessing an encompassing theoretical system. Stevens captured this best in his tribute to Santayana, discussed in the previous chapter, where the familiar metaphor of a theoretical system as a temple links formal closure to repose and permanence:

> Total grandeur of a total edifice,
> Chosen by an inquisitor of structures
> For himself. He stops upon this threshold,
> As if the design of all his words takes form
> And frame from thinking and is realized.[21]

In all these poems from the policeman's side, Stevens reminds us that pleasure does not tempt Equity alone; the proponents of Strict Law are not the ascetic servants of their own legend, but hedonists of another kind. Rhetoric, linking through language the pleasures of thought and feeling, detachment and passion, thus pervades the theoretical life, on its chillier as on its warmer side. There is no theoretical position that cannot appeal, implicitly at least, to "the strong exhilaration / Of what we feel from what we think, of thought / Beating in the heart, as if blood newly came."[22]

Holmes, one of the few prose masters among legal theorists, had made the same point when he ascribed the appeal of classical formalist jurisprudence to "that longing for certainty and for repose which is in every human mind."[23] It does indeed make for a singular romance—this "longing" located not conventionally in the heart but rather in the "mind." And yet when, as always in so inexact a field as law, theories must persuade without demonstrating, and when the very enterprise of explicit theorizing must work against a prejudice in favor of unreflective practice, a theorist's ability to seize the attention by assuaging the mind's longings greatly adds to the theory's chances of success. Holmes's own lasting preeminence in jurisprudence, achieved by brilliant *aperçus* in the absence of an articulated theoretical system, helps make the point. A practical list of prerequisites for a successful working legal theory or supreme legal fiction might well include "It Must Give Pleasure."

Now we must consider the other side. A few years after Stevens wrote his "Russian policeman" journal entry, we find him, in a letter, begging his muse for rescue from the restrictions of even American policemen: "Wild ducks! We followed them. A policeman shouted and we came meekly back to the walk. The police are as thick as trees and as reasonable. But you must obey them.—Now, Ariel, rescue me from police and all that kind of thing."[24] Taking Stevens as a pleasure-giving theoretician, we should turn from his Euclidean, snow-man, Russian-policeman aspect, his poetry of cold order and Strict Law, to his other side: the free spirit, the young poet who felt so intensely the pleasures of spring, warmth, and spontaneity. On Ariel's side, we find a bard of Equity.

To the pleasures of theoretical order, for example, he persuasively opposes the joy of disruptive *spontaneity*. In "Notes," he first portrays the ordered minuet of Alpha and Omega, the "ever-early candor" of realism and the "late plural" of imagination—and then suddenly disrupts them, as "an Arabian in my room" rises from the unconscious with a "damned hoobla-hoobla-hoobla-how" and "throws his stars around." The astrologically lunatic Arabian reminds the poet of the sudden surges of sexual excitement that in his youth could strike from nowhere, when Venus's bird, the wood-dove, "used to chant his hoobla-hoo." And even now, the odd free-associative chain of thought continues, the uncontrollable ocean rejects human ordering with its "grossest iridescence" and "howls hoo and rises and howls hoo and falls." One of Stevens's most privileged words is "pierce," and it is the word he uses to sum up the effect of these disruptions: "Life's nonsense pierces us with strange relation"[25]—just as (the theorist of Equity might say) the world's nonsensical and unforeseeable happenings evade the grid laid across life by the best-designed code of laws, piercing the formal defenses thrown up around the human judge.

To the attractions of intellectual closure, a single system portraying a single Truth, Stevens over and over again responds with a celebration of the world's infinitely rich and open *incompletion*. As I mentioned in the previous chapter, he contrasted to the total grandeur of Santayana's philosophic edifice the creations of a poet named Ariel, who finally "was glad he had written his poems." These poems formed no system, no architectural unity; they were unsystematized reminders of this and that, "of a remembered time / Or of something he liked." Like plants that grew, ripened, and writhed, they would turn to "waste and welter"; but growing together to cover the rock of a single life, they formed their own "planet on the table," bearing "some affluence . . . of the planet of which they were part."[26] In another poem, Stevens makes the same pluralist point, so reminiscent of William James. Perhaps he makes it too explicitly: when the speaker finally recognized that "There is no such thing as the truth" but rather "many truths," then "the silence was largest/ And longest, the night was roundest, / The fragrance of the autumn warmest."[27]

The scientific thinker's characteristic reduction is to seek truth in the correspondence of belief to a hard-edged objective reality that is found behind the variable subjectivity of appearances. Thus, Locke dismissed colors and sounds as "secondary qualities," mere inner and subjective reflections of external and objective (hence "primary") qualities such as extension and mass. Stevens the pluralist and radical empiricist notes what the Lockean "nabob of bones" loses with that reductive epithet "secondary":

> He never supposed
> That he might be truth, himself, or part of it,
> That the things that he rejected might be part
> And the irregular turquoise, part, the perceptible blue
> Grown denser, part, the eye so touched, so played
> Upon by clouds, the ear so magnified
> By thunder, parts, and all these things together,
> Parts, and more things, parts.[28]

Similarly, the champion of Equity takes the view that living law draws on the manifold of experience, its "colors" and subjectivities—not only on the skeleton of an objective reality that can be submitted to formal coding and computation.

Lockean substance with its primary qualities shares an appeal with Platonic Ideas: both are eternal and unchanging, and offer the possibility of certain and impersonal knowledge. But to the formalist appeal of certainty and repose, Stevens's response was constant and insistent: change is *vital*. The permanence of a Platonic heaven of eternal truth is ghostly and unsatisfying because

The greatest poverty is not to live
In a physical world . . .
                                   Perhaps,
After death, the non-physical people, in paradise
Itself non-physical, may, by chance, observe
The green corn gleaming and experience
The minor of what we feel.[29]

The dream of a paradise that is physical and vital and yet free of change, decay, and death is self-contradictory, impossible:

Is there no change of death in paradise?
Does ripe fruit never fall? Or do the boughs
Hang always heavy in that perfect sky,
Unchanging, yet so like our perishing earth . . . ?
. . . . .
Death is the mother of beauty . . .[30]

For Stevens, the "center of time," that still point of the turning world where Heraclitus's river stopped flowing, is "azury,"— blue, imaginary, unreal. If the river is the stream of consciousness, the place where it comes to rest is a place of death, the graveyard of the "man / Of bronze whose mind was made up and who, therefore, died."[31] The equity-minded legal theorist similarly notes that the only really formal and unchanging systems of law are those preserved in books from societies long dead.

Stevens knows the corruptions of coldness as well as its beauties. Chief among them is heartless selfishness, represented by the sweet sinister cold of "The Emperor of Ice-Cream." In the kitchen a cigar-rolling man whips "concupiscent curds" of ice cream as the wenches come and go; in the adjoining bedroom, a dead woman lies in undignified discard, "cold . . . and dumb" under a sheet, her horny feet protruding. Both rooms teach the cynical wisdom that "The only emperor is the emperor of ice-cream": what you see is what you get; look out for Number One; enjoy the sweet cold before the bitter cold claims you.[32] There is no sense of cheerful hedonism or brave existential defiance here. The strange phrase "emperor of ice-cream," especially when joined to the dead woman and the churning arm-movements of the cigar

smoker, recalls the unforgettable image of Dante's Satan, the
"emperor of the realm of pain" ("Lo 'mperador del doloroso
regno"), trapped chest-deep in the ice lake at the bottom of
Hell—ice maintained by the beating of his great batwings.[33]
Contemporary legal theory purchases the pleasures of intellectual
clarity by assuming (and thereby teaching) universal human ego-
ism; the price is a social world modeled on the *doloroso regno* of
economic man.

Cold likewise offers the stoical corruptions of fake tragedy. "In
a Bad Time" critiques the poet who lets "cold's glacial beauty"
tempt him to make "his poverty . . . his heart's strong core," so
that he "struts bare boards," a posturing tragic muse. This is its
own kind of unrealism, "forgetfulness of summer." Obsession
with coldness and imaginative poverty is its own form of narcis-
sism, self-pity, bad acting. The poet must resist the temptation
to dwell entirely with "the muse of misery"; the life-affirming
"purple muse" has claims too.[34] Similarly in legal theory: the sigh
that accompanies recitation of the axioms of universal depravity
too often conceals satisfaction with the order those axioms help
impose.

One poem more than any other sums up for Stevens both the
attractions of cold impersonal thought, and also its inability to
satisfy the needs of a human creature for whom movement, incompletion, groping speech, and imperfection generally, are inseparable from life itself. "The Poems of Our Climate" first sets a
beautiful wintry scene:

> Clear water in a brilliant bowl,
> Pink and white carnations. The light
> In the room more like a snowy air,
> Reflecting snow. A newly-fallen snow
> At the end of winter when afternoons return.

This is a version of the "cold pastoral" of Keats's Grecian urn:

> The day itself
> Is simplified; a bowl of white,

Cold, a cold porcelain, low and round,
With nothing more than the carnations there.

Now suppose the beauty of the scene worked on the spirit to take away for a moment "all one's torment," quieted the ego's hot demands and "made it fresh in a world of white, / A world of clear water, brilliant-edged," like the pleasures of the star-lines at Tallapoosa. This would not be enough:

There would still remain the never-resting mind,
So that one would want to escape, come back
To what had been so long composed.

Then comes the famous line that perhaps best distills the "theory of life" that runs through all Stevens's poetry:

The imperfect is our paradise.

And the conclusion:

Note that, in this bitterness, delight,
Since the imperfect is so hot in us,
Lies in flawed words and stubborn sounds.

In our imperfect paradise, delight *lies* (both senses) in rhetoric: in the flawed words that burst out of the heat of desire to dirty the cold bright-edged silence; in the words that are inevitably false because they never quite capture in their still picture the ever-changing reality that they themselves revise and partly constitute; in the words that are the life of the human world, that world of words to the end of it.

As Richard Weisberg has written, no sphere of life illustrates better than law "the failure of the word."[35] Stevens gives us, with his best Socratic irony, the self-knowledge that this failure is to some degree inevitable. Indeed, the worst deceptions and failures of legal wordiness are nurtured by the impossible (Platonic, Lockean, Cartesian) ideal of discursive transparency, with its inevitably accompanying claim to have realized that ideal in some legal code or system of legal science. Along with the Romantic poet, the legal pragmatist—no irrationalist, but on this subject the tough-minded one[36]—presumes all such claims to be false, and believes that our only attainable paradise will remain imperfect because irreducibly rhetorical.

Conclusion

What Lucretius and Dante teach you . . . is *what it feels like* to
hold certain beliefs.

> —T. S. Eliot
> "The Social Function of Poetry" (1945 version)

Absolutism has a certain *prestige* due to the more radical style of
it.

> —William James, "Pragmatism"

I must now repeat some warnings and specify some disclaimers of
warranty. The connection of Stevens's poetry to legal thought
emerges only from strenuous (though I hope not strained) interpretation. The poet himself rigorously excluded law from the explicit purview of his poems. Moreover, his own declarations of
word and implications of deed, summarized in Chapters II and
III, distance him from the law-and-literature enterprise in its
standard version.

I qualified these negative findings in the foregoing three chapters, but only hypothetically: *if* the poet Stevens speaks to lawyers, it is to teach us pragmatist philosophy. Three separately
formidable barriers stand in the way of fulfilling the hypothesis:
first, we must accept pragmatist philosophy as relevant to law;
second, we must be so drawn to Stevens's poetry that we that we
will work through its initial difficulties to the pragmatism em-
bodied in it; and finally, we must find that this poetry teaches
pragmatism in a way usefully different from the philosophy's
well-known official (prose) expositions.

On the first question, which I have discussed at length elsewhere,[1] I will say here only that pragmatism seems to me the
implicit working legal theory of most good lawyers, though it is

an eminently pragmatic question whether making their pragmatism explicit—articulating it as a theory, a philosophy—can help them as lawyers. I think that for some it can. Take, for example, the challenge posed when another lawyer in the grip of economic analysis, sociobiology, or systems theory says, "I have a scientific legal theory that tells me (and you) what to do." The lawyer or legal scholar who has ready to hand a skeptical pragmatist account of the place of theory can deal articulately with this challenge, where the intuitive or self-consciously antitheoretical lawyer of pragmatist bent is likely to retreat into defensive and rhetorically ineffective irrationalism. And less instrumentally, some lawyers, like some other human beings, theorize in order to give meaning to their working lives by naming and articulating a reasonably satisfying and encompassing general account of their enterprise.

Suppose now you are willing to imagine that pragmatism might mean something to you as a lawyer or legal scholar; how can Wallace Stevens help you? Not at all, unless his poetry gives you pleasure—or joy, to use the traditional Romantic term for poetry's reward, though Stevens himself rarely used it without irony.[2] A surprising number of lawyers do seem to read Stevens, but poetry does not appeal to everyone, and even for poetry readers Stevens poses special difficulties. As Helen Vendler says, his poems are not "first-order," first-person recountings, but "second-order" reflections that "enact the thinking of thoughts, or the sensing of sensations, or the supposing of suppositions (activities for which we do not have the usual narrative plots)."[3]

Even where, rarely, Stevens does speak directly in the first person, he often remains obscure. Take the opening lines of "Montrachet-le-Jardin":

> What more is there to love than I have loved?
> And if there be nothing more, O bright, O bright,
> The chick, the chidder-barn and grassy chives
>
> And great moon, cricket-impresario,
> And, hoy, the impopulous purple-plated past,
> Hoy, hoy, the blue bulls kneeling down to rest.[4]

These lines thrilled as well as baffling me when I first read them. I would not know how to argue anyone into sharing the thrill, yet without it, why struggle through the bafflement? If you do, you come upon another quite wonderful poem on the theme of "Sunday Morning"—the difficult adequacy of the merely natural and contingent in the face of the human yearning for the supernatural and absolute. The lawyer can find in it sustenance similar to that offered by Justice Holmes in a famous essay: we should not be "dissatisfied" at the absence of certification "that our truth is cosmic truth"; our participation in a natural and factual universe gives us "our only but our adequate significance"; after all, "what competent person supposes that he understands a grain of sand?"[5] Stevens, too, proclaims "the grace / and free requiting of responsive fact"; he lets us see "how cataracts / As facts fall like rejuvenating rain," and how "The green fish pensive in green reeds / Is an absolute."[6] The point for the lawyer is made by the title of Holmes's essay: "Natural Law."

Now, finally, suppose that this second barrier has also been passed. The legal reader, attracted to philosophical pragmatism, is drawn to Stevens's poetry as well. The hardest question remains: Why should the reader learn pragmatism from the poems? They add no new propositional content to pragmatist doctrine, which is well articulated elsewhere in good clear prose. Why violate their poetry by treating them as philosophy, plundering them for doctrine, paraphrasing?

The answer lies mostly in pragmatism's peculiar rhetorical disadvantages vis-à-vis other theories. Pragmatism represents the theoretical middle way, and almost by definition it mkes fewer claims than its rivals do. For pragmatists, any theory is only a set of reflections on some existing practice, generated out of and attached to that practice, recognizing its contingency and cultural particularity, and so waiving claims to universal or comprehensive scope. Pragmatism's strength is its rooted and robust character; theory attaches to a going worldly concern, and by claiming no status higher than the practical it avoids the paradoxes of self-reference that plague more ambitious systems.

But its own attractive modesty threatens to usher pragmatism from the philosophical scene. "If you claim so little for your theories, why bother with theorizing at all?" one might ask.[7] Theory as the pragmatist conceives it is no more than articulate reflection sufficiently detached from everyday practice so as to extend premises extracted from that practice, or imported from other practices, beyond their usual limits. This reflective and reflexive critical account of the practice of theorizing sounds question-begging to the standard theorist; its self-imposed practical test (theorize either for fun or profit) invites from those not aesthetically drawn to it insistence on some independent ("genuinely theoretical") criteria by which to identify profit: What makes a change an improvement?

To the request for an evaluative theory that can stand independent of practice and rule over it, pragmatism answers with one of its core propositions: such theories are not to be had. Every theory is a reflection on and of existing practice, or a practice (language game) of its own, and as such subject to further self-reflective adaptation; or else it is some combination of (or alternation between) these. Yet to the unconvinced and theory-starved, this response seems evasive and circular. And to those practicing pragmatists (for example, most lawyers) who think theory of any kind irrelevant because impractical, the answer sounds plausible enough, but tends to confirm that theorizing is not for them.

Hence pragmatism's rhetorical, or public-relations, problem—no trivial matter. Like scientific revolutions, theoretical commitments come typically from *Gestalt* flips, conversion experiences, rarely from proofs and demonstrations alone. Theories that make their mark in the world tend to be bold, sweeping, and dramatic; it is their drama that wins them an audience in the competition for attention. They have the prestige that, as William James noted, attaches to absolutisms.[8] Over the clatter and squeak of everyday practical affairs, a theory will be better heard if it offers either the riveting bang-bang of intellectual entertainment or the stirring trumpet call of spiritual uplift. Of theory as a literary genre, truly may be it be said (shifting the figure to fit the apocalyptic words), "I would thou wert cold or hot." Accordingly, pragmatism, that modest theory of the middle way, will often be rejected: "because thou art lukewarm . . . I will spew thee out of my mouth." [9]

On matters of theory, a primary pragmatist precept—based on the presumed incompleteness of every theory—is familiar to lawyers: "Hear the other side." John Stuart Mill put the point well when he wrote that in the study of society,

> the besetting danger is not so much of embracing falsehood for truth, as of mistaking part of the truth for the whole. It might be plausibly maintained that in almost every one of the leading controversies, past or present, in social philosophy, both sides were in the right in what they affirmed, though wrong in what they denied; and that if either could have been made to take the other's view in addition to its own, little more would have been needed to make its doctrine correct. [10]

But do you not nod off to your own nods of agreement as you hear the good gray liberal expound the mild virtues of golden mediocrity? Like its cognate commandment of lawyerly due process, *Audi alteram partem,* the pragmatist maxim does not stir the blood—no "Love your neighbor as yourself!" or "Give me liberty or give me death!" or "Workers of the world, unite!" Still, what Mill says is true, important, and every day neglected and forgotten, with unhappy practical consequences—just as is the lawyer's Polonius-like advice to hear the other side.

Although it is often put in moral or political terms, I believe that the core objection to the middle way is aesthetic. Bertrand Russell, for example, calls the Aristotelian doctrine of the mean an ethical theory for those "who neither fall below nor rise above the level of decent, well-behaved citizens," the "respectable middle-aged," who use it "to repress the ardors and enthusiasms of the young"; such a theory "to a man with any depth of feeling . . . cannot but be repulsive." [11] This is mostly a stylistic protest invoking the spirit of *avant-garde* modernism: the middle way is mediocre—a cliché, boring, old. Yo! Make it new! Among Russell's contemporaries, Ezra Pound or Emma Goldman could have endorsed his point with equal enthusiasm—which shows its entire lack of moral or political content.

But it is a rhetorically effective message, especially with the best and most high-spirited of the young; though the revulsion against the "lukewarm" is largely aesthetic, the aesthetic qualities of theories are greatly underrated factors in their acceptance or rejection—precisely for the pragmatist reason that theories are so much less demonstrable or refutable than traditional philosophy presupposes. As James put in, victory goes to the theory that is "most completely *impressive.*" [12]

In response to pragmatism's problem of boring moderation, let me for a last time summon Wallace Stevens to the aid of the theoretical middle way.* The poem is "Connoisseur of Chaos," and the problem, which Stevens sets out in mock-scholastic style, is to reconcile two apparently disparate and paradoxical abstractions: "A. A violent order is disorder; and / B. A great disorder is an order." The first part of the poem satirizes Hegelian synthesis ("opposite things partake of one") and concludes: "We cannot go back to that. / The squirming facts exceed the squamous mind, / If one may say so."

Instead, Stevens tries another, distinctively pragmatist form of reconciliation of the generalizations—placing each in a limiting context. Thus, he treats "A" ("A violent order is a disorder") as generalized from "an old order is a violent one" (rigidity requires repression). He then qualifies this as merely "one more truth . . . in the immense disorder of truths"—a qualification that begins to assimilate it to "B" ("a great disorder is an order"). Next, as to "B," he reminds us that the great disorder of the weather never-

---

*I say "theoretic" middle way to make clear that in its approach to practical problems, pragmatism has no necessary tendency to favor complex or compromised solutions over clear-cut or radical ones: it all depends on what the practical needs of the situation require. And how broadly "the situation" is defined is a pragmatic question too. Rigid rules, which are judgments covering broadly defined situations, and extreme outcomes, which entirely reject "the other side," are sometimes just what the context demands. It is *theory-driven* fanatics who most often bring hell to earth.

theless contains the ordered succession of the seasons, an order within random variation around which human life is organized—thus verifying that a great disorder can indeed be an order. Indeed, if the climatic analogy to "the disorder of truths" came to "an order, most Plantagenet, most fixed"—endless summer or winter—it would then be a violent and humanly disordering order, confirming "A," and completing the assigned task of showing that the two generalizations "are one."

The poem to this point has remained something of a riddling logical and linguistic exercise.[13] Stevens saves his most satisfying stroke for the end, as he offers three separate and successive images through which to conceive general principles, or theories, such as his "A" and "B." He begins by stating the first and rejecting it for the second:

> Now, A
> And B are not like statuary, posed
> For a vista in the Louvre. They are things chalked
> On the sidewalk so that the pensive man may see.

Theories understood in the pragmatist ("pensive") way are not Euclidean axioms or Kantian categorical imperatives, but graffiti on the sidewalk, practical guidelines to be put to use by the alertly streetwise when context makes them applicable—a lively and attractive, if not particularly inspiring, picture of the pragmatist conception of theory.

But what *are* we to do for our necessary inspiration? What will be our moral equivalent of war? Inspiration is something an ironic pragmatist like Stevens finds it hard to come by honestly. Yet the poet knows he needs full lungs to sing and is ready to try. He now invites us to picture theories neither as rigid statues (which would suit the temple of his Santayana poem), nor only as perishable graffiti—but as each one a mountain, that emblem of the sublime. The standard top-down theorist will pick out the right mountain, the one true mountain, and go live at the foot of it. Stevens's "pensive" pragmatist is more skeptical of theory, but does not retreat to the flat plains of unreflective practice; rather

> The pensive man . . . He sees that eagle float
> For which the intricate Alps are a single nest.[14]

This, at last, gives to the pragmatic middle way some compensatory and deserved measure of magnificence.

It does more, as well. In another poem, Stevens conceded in good realist fashion that natural objects such as the Alps are "not transformed" by a poet's metaphors, then added: "Yet we are shaken by them as if they were. / We reason about them with a later reason."[15] Legal theorists might well be shaken, and matured into a later reason (or "philosophic mind") by seeing jurisprudence alternately through the frames supplied by Stevens's two metaphors for theorizing—the eagle's survey of mountain peaks and valleys, the street-kid's scrutiny of neighborhood graffiti. And since theories are not natural but cultural objects, they *can* be transformed by such a reconception of the activity that produces them. Re-visioned through the pragmatist lens supplied by Stevens's metaphors, a theory has more in common with a poem than appears from other conceptions of theorizing: it is a fiction, a made thing, a heuristic refreshener, an unstable mixture of the pleasing and the useful.

The eagle's perspective, scanning the multiple peaks of theory, lends elevation to the theorizing enterprise, while the image of the urban graffiti-scanner reminds the theorists at the same time to watch their feet. This does not mean that the two metaphors sharply separate intrinsic (high) from instrumental (low) justifications for theory; the eagle, after all, is probably hunting as well as enjoying the view, and graffiti are often amusing as well as instructive.

Reflection on the two metaphors together recalls the limits imposed by the local and situated character of all theorizing. Jurisprudence is not the same as poetics; the pragmatist Kenneth Burke reminds us that although art and literature are not separate from real life, "one cannot advocate art as a cure for toothache without disclosing the superiority of dentistry."[16] *Law is poetry* is indeed only a metaphor, subject to correction by an indefinite number of other, equally inconclusive metaphors. Law is also *dentistry* (practical gap-filling); but then, too, it is *war,* which means that it is *politics* carried on by other means . . .

To each comparison, a lawyer's response might be captured by these words of Wallace Stevens's: "The metaphor stirred his fear. The object with which he was compared / Was beyond his recognizing." Am I a poet? (A philosopher? An economist? A hired gun?) But the poem goes on:

> By this he knew that likeness of him extended
> Only a little way, and not beyond, unless between himself
> And things beyond resemblance there was this and that
>   intended to be recognized,
> The this and that in the enclosures of hypotheses
> On which men speculated in summer when they were half
>   asleep. [17]

Speculative metaphoric daydreams—surely we lawyers have no room for these within our serious professional jurisdiction. Law is . . . well, law. Yet, continues our poet, in the aptly named "Prologues to What Is Possible," the recognition of "this and that" can with a "flick" add something new and different

> to what is real and its vocabulary,
> The way some first thing coming into Northern trees
> Adds to them all the vocabulary of the South . . .

Thus closes his case, to be reopened at your pleasure.

Abbreviations

Brazeau   Peter Brazeau, *Parts of a World* (New York: Random House, 1983).

CP   *The Collected Poems of Wallace Stevens* (New York: Knopf, 1955).

Letters   Holly Stevens, ed., *Letters of Wallace Stevens* (New York: Knopf, 1966).

NA   Wallace Stevens, *The Necessary Angel* (New York: Vintage, 1951).

OP   Wallace Stevens, *Opus Posthumous,* ed. Milton Bates, 2nd ed. (New York: Knopf, 1989).

Notes

Introduction

1. Richard Posner, *Law and Literature: A Misunderstood Relation* (Cambridge, Mass., 1988), 179. On Kafka as legal authority, see ibid., 176–205, responding to Robin West, "Authority, Autonomy, and Choice: The Role of Consent in the Moral and Political Visions of Franz Kafka and Richard Posner," *Harvard Law Review,* 99 (1986): 384–428.
2. Mark Yudof, "'Tea at the Palaz of Hoon': The Human Voice in Legal Rules," *University of Texas Law Review,* 66 (1988): 592, 593.
3. Margaret Jane Radin, "'After the Final No There Comes a Yes': A Law Teacher's Report," *Yale Journal of Law & the Humanities,* 2 (1990): 253–266. An early 1989 Lexis check showed nineteen citations to Stevens's poetry in the law review database, which goes back to 1982; for what it is worth, he is tied with Auden for the lead in citations among modern poets, the two of them being slightly ahead of Eliot and Frost. At the same time, some literary commentators on Stevens seem to suppose that Stevens's legal training or work as a lawyer bears on his poetry; thus, a valuable recent critical work begins with the observation that the poet Stevens often argues "with the rigor of a good lawyer." Eleanor Cook, *Poetry, Word-Play, and Word-War in Wallace Stevens* (Princeton, 1988), 3.
4. James Boyd White, "The Judicial Opinion and the Poem: Ways of Reasoning, Ways of Life," in White, *Heracles' Bow* (Madison, 1985), 129, 123. Professor White offers an exercise in poetry reading for law students in his law-and-literature textbook, *The Legal Imagination* (Boston, 1973), 761–806. He denies supplying manifestos for a movement—see "Law and Literature: No Manifesto," *Mercer Law Review,* 39 (1988): 739–751—but provides such programmatic pronouncements as "The life of the lawyer is at heart a literary one." *Heracles' Bow,* 77.
5. Robin West, "Economic Man and Literary Woman: One Contrast," *Mercer Law Review,* 39 (1988): 867–887.
6. Ronald Dworkin, "How Law Is Like Literature," in Dworkin, *A Matter of Principle* (Cambridge, Mass., 1985), 146–166; idem, *Law's Empire* (Cambridge, Mass., 1986), 45–86.
7. Posner, *Law and Literature,* 302. He decrees separation subject only to the proviso (303–309) that lawyers can indeed develop their rhetorical skills by reading literature. Professor White responds, in a strongly critical re-

view, that Posner's proviso is "a very small mouse from a very big mountain," and White renews his case for much more extensive assimilation of the legal and literary realms; see White, "Book Review: What Can a Lawyer Learn from Literature?" *Harvard Law Review,* 102 (1989): 2032. Robin West likewise submits Posner's book to fierce attack in "Law, Literature, and the Celebration of Authority," *Northwestern Law Review,* 83 (1989): 977–1011.

8. William James, "Pragmatism," in John McDermott, ed., *The Writings of William James* (Chicago, 1977), 362.

9. A lucid and persuasive statement of the grounds for skepticism about law and literature (as distinguished from Judge Posner's more sweeping rejection of the whole enterprise), written by a former English professor now a legal scholar, is Robert Weisberg, "The Law-Literature Enterprise," *Yale Journal of Law & the Humanities,* 1 (1988): 1–67.

10. Wallace Stevens, "A Poet That Matters," *OP,* 220.

11. I give my conception of the pragmatist revival and its consequences for law in my "Holmes and Legal Pragmatism," *Stanford Law Review,* 41 (1989): 787–870, an expanded version of which is forthcoming from Stanford University Press. Here is the gist of that conception. Pragmatism makes *the practical* central in two senses: it conceives human thought as instrumentally oriented toward achieving practical purposes arising in concrete situations; at the same time, it conceives thought (including theory) as an activity emergent from a context of tacit and culturally constituted practices, rather than as a set of logical operations upon foundational mental elements. Pragmatism regards these practices as subject always to instrumental adaptation through the power of critical reflection; thus, it is not antitheoretical, but rather regards theorizing as itself a situated and instrumental practice or activity, and theories as partial, incomplete, and tentative guides to action and reflection. Among the many influential works that embody the pragmatist revival, I would particularly note Richard Rorty, *Philosophy and the Mirror of Nature* (Princeton, 1979); idem, *Consequences of Pragmatism* (Minneapolis, 1982); and Cornel West, *The American Evasion of Philosophy* (Madison, 1989).

12. Wallace Stevens, "Thirteen Ways of Looking at a Blackbird," *CP,* 92.

13. "Holiday in Reality," *CP,* 313.

14. *OP,* 117.

15. In Shakespeare's "The Phoenix and the Turtle," the conflagration has consumed not only the legendary virgin bird of constancy itself, but also the turtledove, representing love. The confusing fusion leaves "property . . . appalled" and, as in Stevens's poem, "reason . . . confounded." To this paradox, the words of Paul Valéry (whose "Palme" also echoes in "Of Mere Being") seem apposite: a poem "is expressly designed to be born again

from its ashes and to become endlessly what it has just been." Paul Valéry, "Poetry and Abstract Thought," in Valéry, *The Art of Poetry,* trans. Denise Folliot (Princeton, 1958). Finally, Stevens's bird suggests not only the vitalism of the "fire-fangled" phoenix but also (with "gold-feathered") the golden bird figurines that represent "the artifice of eternity" in Yeats's Byzantium poems.

16. John Keats, Letter to George and Thomas Keats, December 21, 1817, in Lionel Trilling, ed., *The Selected Letters of John Keats* (New York, 1951), 92.

I. An Occupation, an Exercise, a Work

1. On the mystery, see the chapter "Stevens as Legend" that introduced the first book-length study of the poet's work, William Van O'Connor, *The Shaping Spirit* (New York, 1950), 3–22. Stevens's friend and long-time professional colleague Wilson Taylor recalls the special curiosity that literature graduate students showed about Stevens's working life at a university seminar he gave in 1973, eighteen years after the poet's death. Wilson Taylor, "Of a Remembered Time," in Frank Doggett and Robert Buttel, eds., *Wallace Stevens: A Celebration* (Princeton, 1980), 91–92.

2. Published primary documents relating to Stevens's life are his *Letters;* and Holly Stevens, ed., *Souvenirs and Prophecies: The Young Wallace Stevens* (New York, 1977), which contains early poems and journals. Peter Brazeau's oral biography *Parts of a World: Wallace Stevens Remembered* is indispensable, particularly on Stevens's daily working and family life. For biographical studies at increasing levels of detail, the reader can consult the excellent essay-length summary in Robert Rehder, *The Poetry of Wallace Stevens* (New York, 1988), ch 1; Milton Bates, *Wallace Stevens: A Mythology of Self* (Berkeley, 1986), a superb one-volume critical biography; and Joan Richardson's two-volume full biography, *Wallace Stevens: The Early Years* (New York, 1986), and *Wallace Stevens: The Later Years* (New York, 1988), which embodies much valuable research.

3. Brazeau, 6.

4. Ibid., 289–290, 291–292.

5. Brazeau, 61–62, 66–67.

6. Ibid., 67; and see 77.

7. Ibid., 51.

8. Thus, he refused interviews and discouraged stories, including a proposed *New Yorker* profile, that might intrude into his working life. *Letters,* 412–415; Brazeau, 47, 56, 67, 68. To O'Connor's *The Shaping Spirit,* Stevens responded by praising the book's exegesis but added "Since that is the part that matters we shall just have to forget the legend." *Letters,* 677.

9. *Letters,* 180, 227, 340.
10. *OP,* 288.
11. See the New York *Times* and *Herald Tribune* obituaries, reproduced in Richardson, *The Later Years* (photo facing 385).
12. John Berryman, "So Long? Stevens," *The Dream Songs* (New York, 1969), 238. Berryman's title alludes contrastively to Walt Whitman's "So Long!" with its famous claim, "this is no book / Who touches this touches a man." *Leaves of Grass* (New York, 1950), 391. Berryman added that Stevens was "better" but "less wide" than himself.
13. The quoted phrase is from Marianne Moore, "Pedantic Literalist," *The Complete Poems of Marianne Moore* (New York, 1967), 37; there is no suggestion that Miss Moore meant it of Stevens.
14. The critical response to Stevens over the course of his career is sampled in Charles Doyle, ed., *Wallace Stevens: The Critical Heritage* (London, 1985); for representative negative views see ibid., 61 (Louis Untermeyer), 70 (Edmund Wilson), 137 (Stanley Burnshaw's Marxist critique), 224 (Yvor Winters's famous "hedonist" essay), 291 (Louise Bogan), 305 (Peter Viereck), and 328 (Randall Jarrell—another famous critique, recanted at 411).
15. An example of Berryman's subtlety is the self-irony in the reference to Stevens as a "grandee crow," which reverses Robert Greene's dismissal of Shakespeare (the ill-educated actor) as an "upstart crow." Greene was a talented but alcoholically short-lived poet whose life sadly presaged Berryman's own. See Stuart Schoenbaum, *Shakespeare's Lives* (New York, 1970), 49–53.
16. W. H. Auden, "In Memory of W. B. Yeats," in Edward Mendelson, ed., *Selected Poems of W. H. Auden* (New York, 1979), 82.
17. Mary McCarthy, *The Groves of Academe* (New York, 1952).
18. When Stevens said to Robert Frost, "The trouble with you is you write about things," Frost riposted, "The trouble with you is you write about bric-a-brac." Stevens told this story on himself (Brazeau, 160).
19. Frank Lentricchia, *Ariel and the Police* (Madison, Wis., 1988), 213. Lentricchia, an insightful reader of Stevens, is ultimately an admirer, but critical both of the canonical understanding of Stevens and of the poet's own self-understanding.
20. Brazeau, 201.
21. Ibid., 193.
22. Book review, *Wallace Stevens Journal,* 8 (1984): 57.
23. Frank Kermode, *Wallace Stevens* (New York, 1960), 1.
24. Bates, *Mythology of Self,* 85.
25. Ibid., 158, 201–203.
26. "Men Made Out of Words," *CP,* 355–356.

27. "Theogony," lines 84–87, in R. M. Frazer, ed. and trans., *The Poems of Hesiod,* (Norman, Okla., 1983), 27. See the discussion in Michael Gagarin, *Early Greek Law* (Berkeley, 1986), 20–26.

28. II Samuel 23: 1–2.

29. Robert Ferguson, *Law and Letters in American Culture* (Cambridge, Mass., 1984), 3–84. But none of the major participants in Ferguson's "configuration" of law and letters was a poet. John Trumbull (ibid., 100–111), was a minor Federalist versifier; and Ferguson's interesting essay on William Cullen Bryant argues that the sense of tension in his best poems depended on his unhappiness with legal practice, which he later abandoned for journalism, to the detriment of American letters (ibid., 173–195).

30. "The poets are the unacknowledged legislators of the world." Percy Bysshe Shelley, "A Defense of Poetry," in Harold Bloom, ed., *Selected Poetry and Prose of Shelley,* (New York, 1966), 448.

31. Matthew Arnold, *Culture and Anarchy* (rpt. New York, 1983), 14–15, 56–58.

32. James Boyd White, *The Legal Imagination,* (Boston, 1973), 757, 761–806; he answers affirmatively in idem, "The Judicial Opinion and the Poem: Ways of Reasoning, Ways of Life," *Heracles' Bow* (Madison, 1985).

33. Brazeau, 27; and see 64.

34. Ibid., 27, 67, 86, 95–96 (delegation); 14, 59, 61–62, 66–67 (avoidance of corporate policy), but see 33; 41 ("prince in principality"), and see 45, 62.

35. The department had one professional and three clerical or secretarial employees in 1924, and had grown to a total of twenty at Stevens's death in 1955. Ibid., 24–25. See ibid., 31, 75–77 (hiring), and 86 (firing).

36. Ibid., 22, 25.

37. Ibid., 20, 23, 39, 57, 77 (hard work); ibid., 34, 41 (perfectionist); ibid., 34, 39; *Letters,* 874 (clean desk).

38. Brazeau, 17, 22, 32, 40, 52.

39. Ibid., e.g., 21, 24, 29, 33, 56, 59, 63–64, 77–78, 85.

40. Wallace Stevens, "Surety and Fidelity Claims," *OP,* 239. The essay (ibid., 237–239) gives a concise description of Stevens's work from his own point of view.

41. Stevens also handled claims on court surety bonds, including bonds on appeals and injunctions, and on executors, administrators, conservators, and guardians. His department also adjusted claims on fidelity bonds, which ensure the honesty of an employee, but as these claims are typically small and routine, Stevens rarely concerned himself with them. See Taylor, "Of a Remembered Time," 342; Brazeau, 25.

42. Brazeau, 24, 57; Taylor, "Of a Remembered Time," 92–93. John Rogers,

the executive row manservant, confirmed the legal character of much of the work: "I've seen Stevens with as many as thirty lawbooks at one time . . . He was a terrific man for legal research." Brazeau, 20. Richard Sunbury, a young man whom Stevens befriended and helped through law school while he worked at the Hartford, recalls Stevens's helping him with his basic law subjects: "he'd give me the focal point to look [for] in each course." Ibid., 36.

43. Taylor, "Of a Remembered Time," 92 ("mercy"); Brazeau, 41, 45 (bend over backward); 41 ("tough as nails"); 29 (indifference to image); 64 (indifference to sales considerations).

44. Taylor, "Of a Remembered Time," 92. Brazeau, 44, 67, 95–96; but see 36.

45. Brazeau, 15; and see 13, 16.

46. Ibid., 67.

47. Ibid., 67, 37.

48. Ibid., 67, 77.

49. In 1942, after more than twenty-five years with the Hartford, he apparently decided to apply for admission to the Connecticut bar; see Wallace Stevens, "Letters to Wilson Taylor," in Doggett and Buttel, eds., *Wallace Stevens*, 80–81. I have not checked to see what came of this plan.

50. Brazeau, 67, 77, 30. None of Stevens's colleagues thought he could have successfully attracted or retained clients, charmed juries, or negotiated successfully with adversaries; these are the basic skills, beyond technical legal knowledge and judgment, on which most practicing lawyers depend to make a living.

51. Taylor, "Of a Remembered Time," 93. Taylor adds that Stevens's time was divided between "strictly legal duties" and work "as an executive of the company."

52. *Paradise Lost*, I, 679–680; and see II, 229–283, for Mammon's speech at the counsel of war in Pandemonium.

53. Walt Whitman, "Song of Myself," Part 42, *Leaves of Grass* (New York, 1950), 64; Marianne Moore, "Poetry," *Complete Poems*, 267.

54. "Livings," "Aubade," in Larkin, *Collected Poems* (London, 1988), 186–188, 208.

55. "Adagia," *OP*, 189, 191. Allen Ginsberg's "American Change," a poetic reflection on a nickel, dime, quarter, five-dollar bill, and one-dollar bill ($6.40), delivers splendidly on Stevens's insight, and even brings in Elsie Stevens, who served as the model for the liberty dime: "Dime next I found, Minerva, sexless cold & chill, ascending goddess of money—and was it the wife of Wallace Stevens, truly?"

56. "Reply to Papini," *CP*, 446–447.

57. "Notes toward a Supreme Fiction," I, iv; *CP*, 383. "We are not at home in / Our interpreted world" ("wir nicht sehr verlässlich zu Haus sind / in

der gedeuteten Welt"): "First Duino Elegy," in Stephen Mitchell, ed. and trans., *Selected Poetry of Rainer Maria Rilke* (New York, 1982). On Stevens's quest for the "normal" and "central," see Chapter IV below.

58. "No Possum, No Sop, No Taters," *CP*, 293.
59. "Evening without Angels," *CP*, 137–138.
60. Brazeau, 184.

II. The Unpeopled World

1. James Boyd White, *Heracles' Bow* (Madison, 1985). John Noonan, *Persons and Masks of the Law* (Cambridge, Mass., 1976), similarly links humanistic approaches to law (there, historical narrative) with humaneness. The common ground of all law-and-literature work is opposition to scientism and formalism in law.

2. For doubts about linguistic theories, see Robin West, "Adjudication Is Not Interpretation: Some Reservations about the Law and Literature Movement," *Tennessee Law Review,* 54 (1987): 203–278; idem, "Communities, Texts, and Law: Reflections on the Law and Literature Movement," *Yale Journal of Law & the Humanities,* 1 (1988): 129–156; Robert Cover, "Violence and the Word," *Yale Law Journal,* 95 (1986): 1601–1629. For advocacy of psychological theories, see Robin West, "Economic Man and Literary Woman: One Contrast," *Mercer Law Review,* 39 (1988): 867–887; Robert Cover, "*Nomos* and Narrative," *Harvard Law Review,* 97 (1983): 4–68. For the theme of pluralism and the voice of the excluded, see the symposium "Legal Storytelling," *Michigan Law Review,* 87, no. 8 (1989).

3. Into this category would go Foucault-influenced and deconstruction-influenced law-and-literature writing, of which there has not been much. One masterful deconstructive literary study, relevant to law but apparently (and instructively?) written innocent of any intent to educate lawyers about their business, is Barbara Johnson, "Melville's Fist: The Execution of *Billy Budd,*" in Johnson, *The Critical Difference* (Baltimore, 1980), 79–109.

4. Holly Stevens, ed., *Souvenirs and Prophecies: The Young Wallace Stevens* (New York, 1977), 50, 48; and see 52, the entry of the day following: "There is too confounded much natural splendor here, however, to allow me to feel deeply the human destitution." Richard Ellmann takes the "I am too cold" entry as the starting point for a thoughtful biographical essay, arguing that Stevens later came to terms with his own detachment through the reductive celebration of coldness in his poetry, represented by poems like "The Snow Man" and "The Emperor of Ice Cream"—a theme I discuss in Chapter VI. Richard Ellmann, "How Wallace Stevens Saw Himself," in Frank Doggett and Robert Buttel, eds., *Wallace Stevens: A Celebration,* (Princeton, 1980), 159, 163–166.

5. Brazeau, 56. Corn was the "Naaman" of "Certain Phenomena of Sound," *CP*, 286–287.

6. *Letters,* 795.

7. "Esthétique du Mal," xii, *CP*, 323.

8. *Letters,* 125.

9. Ibid., 458, 391.

10. Brazeau, 251. Around this time, Stevens wrote to his niece, on the subject of his own father, words that could have been autobiographical: he "needed what all of us need, and what most of us don't get: that is to say, discreet affection. So much depends on ourselves in that respect. I think that he loved to be at the house with us, but he was incapable of lifting a hand to attract any of us, so that, while we loved him as it was natural to do, we were afraid of him, at least to the extent of holding off. The result was that he lived alone." *Letters,* 454.

11. For testimony portraying Wallace Stevens as a long-suffering victim of his wife's neurosis, see, among many passages, Brazeau, 21, 26, 80, 157–158, 232–235 (Mrs. Stevens found it impossible to keep servants; as a result, after the mid-thirties, Wallace Stevens took on the task of washing the dishes and scrubbing the floors —see *Letters,* 450n.), 243, 245–247, 252–253; and the report of Holly Stevens, who uses the term "persecution complex," in *Souvenirs and Prophecies,* 137, supplemented at second hand in Brazeau, 286–287. For suggestions pointing the other way, toward Elsie Stevens as victim of her husband's isolating persecution, an unhappy Mme Teste, see Brazeau, 81, 133, 175, 187, 248–249, 250–251.

12. Brazeau, 207–208, 235.

13. His closest friend for a number of years was the philanthropist Henry Church, to whom he dedicated "Notes toward a Supreme Fiction," and for whom "The Owl in the Sarcophagus" is an elegy. But the two men rarely saw each other. The *Letters* likewise record his almost entirely epistolary friendships with Hi Simons, José Rodríguez Feo, and others. In his last years Stevens did become friends with, and saw fairly often, the young Hartford poet Samuel French Morse; Brazeau, 151–160.

14. The letters, sadly, are lost. See Brazeau, 94–109, for a record of the friendship; Brazeau calls Powell "one of those rare individuals who made Stevens's world a more human place."

15. Brazeau, 62; and see to the same effect 72, 160, 247. Perhaps Stevens's closest work friend was Ralph Mullen, his assistant for thirty years; Brazeau, 245–247. For other close work friendships see ibid., 75–81 (Anthony Sigmans); ibid., 249–251 (Manning Heard); 84–88, and Taylor, "Of a Remembered Time" (Wilson Taylor); Brazeau, 88–93 (James Powers, plus his wife Margaret, the "Jim and Margaret" of "A Fish-Scale Sunrise," *CP*, 160; Margaret Powers gives perhaps the warmest and most at-

tractive human portrait we have of Wallace Stevens). See, for other Stevens work friendships, Brazeau, 40–44 (Charles O'Dowd), and 44–45 (A. J. Fletcher, who "just loved the fellow").

16. Brazeau, 266–271 (Jane MacFarland Wilson: the friendship was "the best thing that had happened to me. . . it was love at first sight"); ibid., 278–282 (Anna May Stevens: "I just adored Uncle Wallace").

17. Ibid., 252, 285.

18. Ibid., 34–39. To a similar effect is the testimony of John Rogers, the black manservant to the company executives, later a history professor (ibid., 34–39); and that of Hazel Kuhnly, a secretary who approached Stevens to show him some poetry she had written, (ibid., 49–50).

19. Joan Richardson, *Wallace Stevens: The Later Years* (New York, 1988), 141–142.

20. Ibid., 96.

21. The writing lapse resulted not only from infant distractions (see *Letters,* 249), but also, perhaps, from a sense of creative exhaustion. To Stevens, the poems of *Harmonium,* still probably the favorites of most of his readers, seemed "horrid cocoons from which later abortive insects have sprung . . . [they are] outmoded and debilitated poems." His only recourse seemed "rather desperately to keep on dabbling and to be as obscure as possible until I have perfected an authentic and fluent speech for myself." *Letters,* 231. This perhaps explains the self-canceling tone of "The Comedian as the Letter C" (*CP,* 27–46), one of Stevens's last major efforts before the six-year silence.

22. Harold Bloom, *Wallace Stevens: The Poems of Our Climate* (Ithaca, 1976), 89.

23. "So-and-So Reclining on a Couch," *CP,* 295–296.

24. Made explicit, in my opinion unsuccessfully, in "The Comedian as the Letter C."

25. As to which, see Philip Larkin, "Deceptions": "What can be said,/ Except that suffering is exact, but where / Desire takes charge, readings will grow erratic?" Larkin, *Collected Poems* (London, 1988), 32.

26. In addition to legal writers such as Robin West, others who have recently written persuasively on behalf of the use of narrative in moral and political argument and education include Richard Rorty, *Contingency, Irony, and Solidarity* (Cambridge, 1989); and Wayne Booth, *The Company We Keep* (Berkeley, 1988). Shelley claimed the same sympathy-expanding virtues for poetry: "The great secret of morals is love; or a going out of our own nature . . . A man, to be greatly good, must imagine intensely and comprehensively . . . Poetry enlarges the circumference of the imagination by replenishing it with thoughts of ever new delight . . . [and thus] strengthens the faculty which is the organ of the moral nature of man, in the same manner as exercise strengthens a limb." Percy Bysshe Shelley, "A

Defense of Poetry," in Harold Bloom, ed., *Selected Poetry and Prose of Shelley* (New York, 1966), 424–425.

27. "Of Modern Poetry," *CP,* 239–240. Compare "Adagia," *OP,* 191: "To read a poem should be an experience, like experiencing an act."

28. *Wallace Stevens: Words Chosen Out of Desire* (Cambridge, Mass., 1986), 32, and passim.

29. "Saint John and the Back-Ache," *CP,* 437. Behind the abyss, the poem goes on to reveal, may be a serpent whose bite will make love go "limp with age." Another subject in many of Stevens's nominally epistemological passages is his longing for a replacement for the lost religious faith of his childhood, as expressed in his essay "Two or Three Ideas," *OP,* 260: "To see the gods dispelled in mid-air and dissolve like clouds is one of the great human experiences . . . It was their annihilation, not ours, and yet it left us feeling that in a measure, we, too, had been annihilated. It left us feeling dispossessed and alone in a solitude, like children without parents, in a home that seemed deserted." That Stevens succumbed to this nostalgia for his gods or God with a deathbed conversion to Catholicism seems likely, though the facts are contested. See Brazeau, 290–291, 294–296, 310; and compare Milton Bates, *Wallace Stevens: A Mythology of Self* (Berkeley, 1986), 296–297, with Helen Vendler, "The Hunting of Wallace Stevens," in Vendler, *The Music of What Happens* (Cambridge, Mass., 1988), 80.

30. *CP,* 240–241.

31. *CP,* 454.

32. *CP,* 413. The poem portrays a solitary poet confronting a beautiful but alien and terrifying nature, northern lights and north wind, as night falls and winter comes to a lonely cabin on a beach.

33. *CP,* 406–407.

34. "John Crowe Ransom: Tennessean," *OP,* 248.

35. See, e.g., Helen Vendler, *On Extended Wings: Wallace Stevens's Longer Poems* (Cambridge, Mass., 1969), 118, 263; Bloom, *Poems of Our Climate,* 117–118. Frank Lentricchia's lengthy political discussion of Stevens in *Ariel and the Police* (Madison, 1988) is not really contrary; Lentricchia thinks Stevens a great poet and his poetry and life together a politically instructive phenomenon, but does not argue that his self-consciously sociopolitical poetry is important or successful. Since this was written, the Fall 1989 issue of *The Wallace Stevens Journal* appeared, devoted to the theme "Stevens and Politics"; several of the essays are of real biographical interest, but none of them leads me to change the judgment expressed in the text.

36. See Stanley Burnshaw, "Turmoil in the Middle Ground," *New Masses* 17 (October 1935): 41–42, reprinted in Charles Doyle, ed., *The Critical Her-*

itage (London, 1985), 137–140. The most trenchant statement of the general anti-Symbolist point—it stands up remarkably well after nearly sixty years—was Edmund Wilson, *Axel's Castle* (New York, 1931), 257–298, which Stevens had read; see *Letters*, 357.

37. *OP*, 75–101. Stevens extensively paraphrased the poem (*Letters*, 366–375); Helen Vendler analyzes it (*On Extended Wings*, 79–118); Milton Bates puts it in its cultural-political context (*Mythology of Self*, 165–184).

38. *CP*, 273–281.

39. Wallace Stevens, *The Palm at the End of the Mind*, ed. Holly Stevens (New York, 1967), 203; "The Noble Rider and the Sound of Words," *NA*, 19–23. See also the earlier statement concerning the "pressure of the contemporaneous" on the poet during the Depression in "The Irrational Element in Poetry" (1937), *OP*, 229.

40. *CP*, 97. See the interesting treatment of this poem, and Stevens's First World War poetry generally, in James Longenbach, "The 'Fellowship of Men that Perish': Wallace Stevens and the First World War," *The Wallace Stevens Journal*, 13 (1989): 85–108. The very short but moving "Flyer's Fall" (*CP*, 336), written during the Second World War, also treats death in war as natural death. And Stevens's important long poem "Esthétique du Mal" (*CP*, 313–326), written in 1944 partly in response to complaints about poets' irrelevance in wartime (see *Letters*, 468), explores not so much moral or political evil, but, exploiting the ambiguity of the French word *mal*, suffering in the face of natural processes.

41. Which Stevens parodied by way of the "Concerto for Airplane and Pianoforte," that "newest Soviet reclame," in the "Duck for Dinner" section of "Owl's Clover" (*OP*, 93–94).

42. See for an excellent contemporary statement of the democratic and pragmatist Emerson-Whitman-Dewey position, with discussion of Stevens, Richard Poirier's *The Renewal of Literature* (New York, 1987).

43. Thus, in an early journal entry, Stevens denounced "art for art's sake" as "the most arrant as it is the most inexcusable rubbish"; art must "perpetuate inspiration or thought" and must "fit with other things." *Letters*, 24. His Whitmanian communal and democratic aspects appear in the penultimate ("chant in orgy") stanza of "Sunday Morning" and in "Anecdote of the Jar," as Frank Lentricchia argues (*Ariel and the Police*, 166–167, 5–20); Harold Bloom stresses the Emerson-Whitman influence throughout *Poems of Our Climate;* and Richard Poirier gives his different placement of Stevens in this tradition in *The Renewal of Literature*, 204–223. For a full-dress comparative study of those two superficially most dissimilar poets, see Diane Middlebrook, *Walt Whitman and Wallace Stevens* (Ithaca, 1974).

44. "Noble Rider," *NA*, 27; "Effects of Analogy," *NA*, 121–122; *OP*, 253.

45. "I have the greatest respect for [William Carlos Williams], although there

is the constant difficulty that he is more interested in the way of saying things than in what a writer has to say. The fact remains that we are always fundamentally interested in what a writer has to say." *Letters*, 544; and cf. ibid., 803.

46. *OP*, 254; "Noble Rider," *NA*, 29; "Adagia," *OP*, 193. One of Stevens's favorites among his own poems, "Large Red Man Reading" (*CP*, 423–424), illustrates his conception of poetry's healing function. Ghosts who had "expected more" of "the wilderness of stars" return to earth to listen to a poet read "from the poem of life / Of the pans above the stove, the pots on the table, the tulips among them." Long deprived of these Dutch physicalities, they "laughed, as he sat there reading" because he "spoke the feeling for them, which was what they had lacked." For a gloss expressing Stevens's doubts at his capacity to supply this sort of "normal" and life-refreshing poetry, see *Letters*, 642–643.

47. Rorty, *Contingency, Irony, and Solidarity*, 83–95.

48. J. S. Mill, "Bentham" and "Coleridge," in Mill, *Utilitarianism and Other Essays*, ed. Alan Ryan (London, 1987), 132–226. Mill's essay on Bentham also suggests what Rorty, with his distrust of systematic thought, tends to leaves out—the importance of institutional design, economic analysis, and social science, as well as heightened empathy, in achieving a society whose central value is resistance to suffering. The literary tend to know only Foucault's Bentham, the inventor of the Panopticon; the version drawn by Mill, well-known for his own personal anti-Benthamite rebellion, is a valuable corrective.

49. Stevens was a middle-of-the-roader in politics, mildly right of center. He left his family's traditional affiliation to become a Republican and favored Eisenhower over Stevenson in 1952 (Brazeau, 278, 153); believed in a vague and unspecified pro-worker "up to date capitalism" that made him think he was "headed left" during the thirties, when he would have "experimented a little more extensively" in public ownership, but opposed talk of "exploitation," and favored the AFL over the CIO (*Letters*, 286, 292, 351; Brazeau, 123); expressed some equivocal sympathy for Mussolini at the same time (Brazeau, 289, 295); defended Pétain's role in the Vichy government (*Letters*, 573); complained about the income tax (*Letters*, 528, 763; "Noble Rider," *NA*, 21); was always strongly anticommunist ("Imagination as Value," *NA*, 143; *Letters*, 286, 350, 515, 532, 620); thought that if William Carlos Williams had made anti-American statements he could properly be dropped as poetry consultant to the Library of Congress (*Letters* 768); and uncritically practiced the casual racism and anti-Semitism that was typical (though by no means universal) among those of his class and period (*Letters*, 286; Brazeau, 82–83, 196, 249, 277).

50. "Owl's Clover," *OP*, 80.
51. Villiers de l'Isle-Adam, "Axel," quoted in Wilson, *Axel's Castle*, 263.
52. "Two or Three Ideas," *OP*, 262; see also "Imagination as Value" (*NA*, 133), to the effect that imagination is no more intrinsically trustworthy than is reason or human nature itself.
53. "Poetry Is a Destructive Force," *CP*, 192–193. Compare "A Weak Mind in the Mountains," *CP*, 212—"There was the butcher's hand. / He squeezed it and the blood / Spurted from between the fingers / And fell to the floor. / And then the body fell"—with *Letters*, 459, speaking of Van Gogh's "total subjection of reality to the artist," and adding "that is so often what one wants to do in poetry: to seize the whole mass of everything and squeeze it, and make it one's own." Denis Donoghue speculates thoughtfully on the tendency toward political authoritarianism of Romantic poets in *W. B. Yeats* (New York, 1971), 131–138.
54. Walter Benjamin, "The Work of Art in the Age of Mechanical Reproduction," in Benjamin, *Illuminations* (New York, 1969), 241.
55. "Extracts from Addresses to the Academy of Fine Ideas," *CP*, 253. Rorty supplies interesting and persuasive readings of Nabokov and Orwell on the dangers of moral aestheticism (*Contingency, Irony, and Solidarity*, 141–188); and Clifford Geertz writes brilliantly to the same effect, using Balinese suttee as his example ("Found in Translation: On the Social History of the Moral Imagination," in Geertz, *Local Knowledge* [New York, 1983], 36–54). Stevens almost surely knew William James's celebrated portrayal of the aesthetic and spiritual attractions of the military spirit in "The Moral Equivalent of War," which I suspect supplied at least part of the inspiration for his poem "Chocorua to Its Neighbor," *CP*, 296–302 (James had had a summer house at Chocorua).
56. *CP*, 446–447.
57. Benjamin, "Work of Art," 241–242.
58. Brazeau, 88.
59. Louis Martz, "Wallace Stevens: The World as Meditation," in Marie Borroff, ed., *Wallace Stevens: A Collection of Critical Essays,* (Englewood Cliffs, N.J., 1963), 147.

III. Fat Cat, Ghostly Rabbit

1. "The use of words in connotative senses was denounced by Locke and Hobbes, who desired a mathematical plainness: in short, perspicuous words." "Noble Rider," *NA*, 13. Hobbes wrote: "The light of human minds is perspicuous words, but by exact definitions first snuffed and purged from ambiguity . . . Metaphors and senseless and ambiguous words are like *ignes fatui* [will-o'-the-wisps]; and reasoning upon them is

wandering among innumerable absurdities; and their end, contention and sedition, or contempt." *Leviathan,* pt. I, ch. 5.

2. John Locke, *An Essay Concerning Human Understanding,* bk. III, ch. X, para. 34.

3. The development of Romanticism as a literary, philosophical, and (to a lesser extent) social and political movement is traced in M. H. Abrams's two great studies, *The Mirror and the Lamp* (New York, 1953) and *Natural Supernaturalism* (New York, 1971). Roberto Unger, *Passion* (New York, 1975), and idem, *Politics, a Work in Constructive Social Theory* (Cambridge, 1987), constitute a contemporary *political* restatement of radical Romanticism.

4. Clifford Geertz, "Local Knowledge: Fact and Law in Comparative Perspective," in *Local Knowledge* (New York, 1983), 172, 174.

5. For a brief theoretical statement of the theory of this point, with references to examples of its practice, see Robin West, "Economic Man and Literary Woman: One Contrast," *Mercer Law Review,* 39 (1988): 739–751.

6. See Patricia Williams, "The Obliging Shell: An Informal Essay on Formal Equal Opportunity," *Michigan Law Review,* 87 (1989): 2128–2151; and Mari Matsuda, "Looking to the Bottom: Critical Legal Studies and Reparation," *Harvard Civil Rights–Civil Liberties Law Review,* 22 (1987): 323–356.

7. See J. M. Balkin, "Deconstructive Practice and Legal Theory," *Yale Law Journal,* 96 (1987): 743–786.

8. James Boyd White, *Heracles' Bow,* (Madison, 1985), 118.

9. James Boyd White, *The Legal Imagination,* (Boston, 1973), 761–762 (quoting Sidney, Emerson, and Coleridge.)

10. "The style of a poem and the poem itself are one." "Two or Three Ideas," *OP,* 257.

11. *Letters,* 413–414.

12. "Poetry and surety claims aren't as unlikely a combination as they may seem. There is nothing perfunctory about them, for each case is different." Quoted in Milton Bates, *Wallace Stevens: A Mythology of Self* (Berkeley, 1986), 157.

13. *Letters,* 792.

14. "Description without Place," *CP,* 345.

15. "An Ordinary Evening in New Haven," xii, *CP,* 473–474.

16. "Men Made Out of Words," *CP,* 355.

17. *CP,* 165.

18. Decades ago, the distinguished legal theorist and critic of positivism Lon Fuller inserted a typed copy of these lines in one of his books to back up a critique of the central positivist distinction between the real law that is

and the imagined natural law that ought to be. Kenneth Winston, "Is/ Ought Redux: The Pragmatist Context of Lon Fuller's Conception of Law," *Oxford Journal of Legal Studies,* 8 (1988): 339.

19. Stevens did work on poetry at the office when time allowed, and kept the results in the "lower right corner of his desk, which was open most of the time to a degree." Brazeau, 38; and see ibid., 23.
20. *Letters,* 494.
21. Brazeau, 62 (Harry Williams).
22. Ibid., 44.
23. Ibid., 14 (Robert De Vore). On the straightforward and concise character of Stevens's legal letters, see also ibid., 28 (Clifford Burdge), 56 (Herbert Schoen), 89 (Margaret Powers), 96 (Elliot Goldstein).
24. Wilson Taylor, "Of a Remembered Time," in Frank Doggett and Robert Buttel, eds., *Wallace Stevens: A Celebration* (Princeton, 1980), 93, 96. Richard Sunbury reported "he was a master of metaphor" (ibid., 37); and Charles O'Dowd, who read his letters as a professional duty, used to copy passages from them for his own amusement and instruction (ibid., 40).
25. See, e.g., *Letters,* 477 (letter to Henry Church about his will); ibid., 516–517 (letter discussing the treason charge against Ezra Pound); "Surety and Fidelity Claims," *OP,* 237–239. Stevens's essay "Insurance and Social Change" (ibid., 233–237) is not of this character; it is, rather, an exercise in deadpan Stevensian comedy, stimulated by the claim he found in one of his company's bulletins to agents: "Cemeteries have been found by a number of offices to be a very definite market for the Hartford's All Risk Securities Policy." He takes the occasion for some ironic and fanciful graveyard-of-capitalism reflections on international trends toward socialism and government-sponsored social insurance.
26. *CP,* 10, 59, 27, 260, 349, 75.
27. Ibid., 40.
28. Ibid., 28.
29. "Three Academic Pieces," *NA,* 71.
30. Ibid., 76. If I may translate, Stevens is making the nominalist point that resemblances do not announce themselves to perception, but must be imposed by the mind—or, what is the same thing in practice, selected for attention from among the infinity of preexisting resemblances that reality makes available.
31. *Letters,* 874.
32. *OP,* 197.
33. *OP,* 253.
34. "Notes toward a Supreme Fiction," I, ix, *CP,* 388. The quoted canto traces the lineage of Stevens's supreme poet or major man back to his earlier image of the subconscious, or sub-man ("Owl's Clover," *OP,* 75–

78). Later this figure, reshaped as a collective unconscious or imagination, something like Shelley's "spirit of the age," will change into the
"spectre of the spheres" of "The Auroras of Autumn" (vii, *CP*, 417), and
the "dauntless master" of "Puella Parvula" (*CP*, 456).

35. "The Figure of the Youth as Virile Poet," *NA*, 57–58.

36. *Letters*, 761.

37. *Letters*, 356. See also ibid., 305: "Poetry must limit itself in respect to
intelligence. There is a point at which intelligence destroys poetry."

38. *CP*, 209–210. The reversing of "natural" symbolism adds to the strange
effect of the poem; rabbits seem quotidian creatures, and (Eliot's practical
cats aside) poets have generally treated cats as creatures of mystery, night,
the moon.

39. See "Anecdote of the Prince of Peacocks," *CP*, 57–58: "In the moonlight /
I met Berserk"; this prince of Madness warns "I set my traps / In the midst
of dreams," inspiring "dread" in the "beauty / Of the moonlight." And
compare "The unspotted imbecile revery . . . The amorist adjective af-
lame" of the unchecked imagination in "Blue Guitar," xiii, *CP*, 172.

40. "To the One of Fictive Music," *CP*, 88.

41. *Letters*, 252. The milk and moonlight reappeared, with the same import,
in the arch "Les Plus Belles Pages," *CP*, 244. In "The Candle a Saint" (*CP*,
223), Stevens returned to the rabbit and cat in an awkwardly forced effort
to transcend their opposition. Green night, the "abstract, the archaic
queen," is both imagined (female, nocturnal) and real (she "walks among
astronomers"); this Lady Aufhebung "strides above the rabbit and the cat"
in the eye of the poet, who thus "sees, beyond the astronomers."

42. *Letters*, 426.

43. Ibid., 28.

44. Ibid., 767.

45. Ibid., 659; see also 776, 799.

46. "Notes toward a Supreme Fiction," *CP*, 405. Earlier in the same poem
Stevens had satirized the romanticization of bird song—Keats's, Shelley's, and Whitman's nightingale, skylark, mockingbird, and thrush
(ibid., 393–394); here he celebrates its humble and domestic virtues.
Helen Vendler reads the passage quoted as no celebration but a "deadened
statement," portraying by its halting punctuation a "laborious . . . tread-
mill"; however, she stops her quotation of the passage short of the line
about wine coming in a wood, which to my ear establishes a more affirmative tonality. Helen Vendler, *On Extended Wings: Wallace Stevens's Longer
Poems* (Cambridge, Mass., 1969), 201–202. The poem alludes to and
joins the great tradition of poetic celebrations of cyclicity; as Richard
Rorty reminds me, the deliberate choice of philosophical terminology
("final in itself, and therefore good") particularly echoes scholastic doc-

trines of circular heavenly revolution as symbolic of self-sufficient good, and so invokes the last lines of the *Divine Comedy*, the ultimate vision of perfected human existence as eternal revolution driven by divine love, "ma gia volgeva il mio disio e *velle*, / si come rota ch'igualmente e mossa, / l'amor che move il sole e l'altre stelle" ("But my / desire and will were moved already—like / a wheel revolving uniformly—by / the Love that moves the sun and the other stars").

47. *Letters*, 431.
48. Taylor, "Of a Remembered Time," 92. Taylor quoted Stevens's adage: "I have no life except in poetry. No doubt that would be true if my whole life was free for poetry" (*OP*, 200); the second sentence lends the adage a proper Stevensian ambiguity, with ironic possibilities. See *Letters*, 644: "Repetition . . . is deadly. But, then, so too is a life without the need of a job." And compare *Letters*, 669.
49. *Letters*, 852–853. Philip Larkin's second ode to "the toad, work" probably applies to Stevens too: "Give me your arm, old toad; / Help me down Cemetery Road." Larkin, "Toads Revisited," *Collected Poems* (London, 1988), 148.
50. *Letters*, 716 (emphasis added).
51. Brazeau, 26, where it is also reported Stevens died intestate in 1955, leaving an estate valued (conservatively) at just under $100,000.
52. In what follows, I am especially indebted to Frank Lentricchia's discussion of Stevens in his *Ariel and the Police*. (Madison, 1988).
53. *Letters*, 180.
54. Holly Stevens, ed., *Souvenirs and Prophecies: The Young Wallace Stevens* (New York, 1977), 71 (emphasis deleted).
55. *Letters*, 171 (1911: "my trifling poesies are like the trifling designs one sees on fans"), 231 (1922: "my earlier things seem like horrid cocoons from which later abortive insects have sprung"), 760 (1952: of his *Selected Poems*, "book seemed rather slight and small to me—and unbelievably irrelevant to our actual world"). In the next chapter, I discuss and document Stevens's incessant yearning for the "normal" and the "central" in his poetry.
56. *CP*, 128–130, 520, 524; see also the invocation beginning "Notes toward a Supreme Fiction" (*CP*, 380), for another representation of the interiorized muse. Adrienne Rich exclaimed of "The Idea of Order at Key West," "If that poem had been written by a woman, my God!" See "Interview," in Albert Gelpi and Barbara Charlesworth Gelpi, eds., *Adrienne Rich's Poetry* (New York, 1975), 116.
57. Brazeau, 56.
58. Stevens strove to an almost obsessive degree to keep all taint of money *out* of his poetic world; he invariably returned speaking honorariums and

payments from magazines for poems, and constantly urged young poets to keep their money making separate from their poetry. That was one reason he disapproved of university teaching as a way for a poet to earn a living. Herbert Schoen reported that "he thought other poets who had chairs in universities or read to women's groups or men's groups were kept men." Brazeau, 56; and see ibid., 167, 172, 186n. (on fees and honorariums); 145, 173, 197 (on earning a separate living).

59. Ibid., 32–33, 69–71, 73–75, 78–79, 153.

60. Stevens's father pushed him into the law when he wanted to pursue a writer's career in New York; see *Letters*, 34, 52–53. Responding to the paternal voice (see "Notes," III, ix), Stevens praised the male bird that "bugles for the mate, nearby the nest," and ended the canto with the suggestion that "Perhaps, / The man-hero is not the exceptional monster, / But he that of repetition is the most master." *CP*, 405–406. Implementing these values, Stevens declined to appear at Dylan Thomas's memorial, commenting privately in a letter that Thomas was "an utterly improvident person" who spent his money "without regard to his responsibilities." *Letters*, 802. He then engaged in fund raising and legal work for the support of Thomas's widow (Brazeau, 57).

61. Blaise Pascal, *Thoughts*, no. 307 (Garden City, N.Y., n.d.).

62. *NA*, 134.

63. Ibid.

64. "Two or Three Ideas," *OP*, 262.

IV. Steel against Intimation

1. *CP*, 288.

2. The noon sun as a metaphoric vehicle for law was no doubt familiar to Stevens from Valéry's "noontime the just" with its "pitiless blades." "Midi le juste y compose de feux / La mer, la mer, toujours recommencée! . . . Je te soutiens, admirable justice / De la lumière aux armes sans pitié!" (Slightly modifying David Paul's translation, "Noontime the just compounds with fires / The sea, the sea, perpetually renewed! . . . I can withstand you, admirable justice / Of light itself, with your pitiless blades!") "Le Cimetière Marin," in James Lawler, ed., *Paul Valéry: An Anthology* (Princeton, 1977), 268–271.

3. Oliver Wendell Holmes, Jr., "Law in Science—Science in Law," *Collected Legal Papers* (New York, 1920), 238. It is not only a lawyer's fantasy to find these legal resonances in the poem; literary commentators hear similar overtones. Thus, Patricia Parker describes the poem's place of reality as "the noonday sun of a Mammon world of industry, stenolanguage, and fixed identities," a place dominated by "the hard certainties, and resolute end-directedness, of Men of Power." Parker, "The Motive for Metaphor:

Stevens and Derrida," *Wallace Stevens Journal,* 7 (1983): 81. Helen Vendler
identifies it not only with a smithy but also with a place of execution; she
finds the "sharp flash" to be "surgical," as it evokes for her the finality of
the executioner's blade. Vendler, *Words Chosen Out of Desire* (Cambridge,
Mass., 1986), 24–25.

4. *Letters,* 352.
5. Ibid. He took up the challenge in the charmingly self-deprecating "A Lot
of People Bathing in a Stream," *CP,* 371. The poet goes for an outing "in
the company of the sun / Good-fortuner of the grotesque," and swims,
naked, amid "addicts / To blotches, angular anonymids" as they "bathed
. . . and dangled down." Once the *rite de passage* ("passing a boundary")
of this slumming expedition was over, "How good it was at home again
at night," in familiar rooms "which do not ever seem to change."
6. *Letters,* 521; "Effects of Analogy," *NA,* 122. In 1949, he again noted his
desire to write poems of "normal life, insight into the commonplace, reconciliation with every-day reality." He was "happy" when he could write
such poems, but, he added wistfully, "it is not possible to get away from
one's own nature" (*Letters,* 642–643). For other letters expressing Stevens's urge to achieve the "normal" or "central," see ibid., 711, 740, 760;
for comments by Stevens on his own obscurity, some defensive in character, see *Letters,* 403, 710, 873; for discussions of the "normality" issue in
his lectures, see "Effects of Analogy," *NA,* 115–116; "Imagination as
Value," *NA,* 153–156. At the end of his life, in one of his last poems, "As
You Leave the Room" (*OP,* 116–117), Stevens was still fighting the fear
that he had been a marginal "skeleton" or "disbeliever in reality," and
alluded to a number of his efforts at red-blooded poetry.
7. In a letter of December 8, 1942, Stevens reports having sent "The Motive
for Metaphor" to the magazine *Chimera,* where it was published in 1943.
Letters, 430.
8. "Noble Rider," *NA,* 34–35.
9. *Letters,* 408.
10. *CP,* 407–408.
11. Compare the more sophisticated treatment in "Notes," II, ix, where Stevens portrays himself as fluctuating between "the poet's gibberish" and
"the gibberish of the vulgate" (*CP,* 396–397).
12. Cf. James Merrill:"'How gladly with proper words,' said Wallace Stevens,
/ 'The soldier dies.' Or kills." Merrill, *Late Settings* (New York, 1985), 26.
Frank Lentricchia captures Stevens's problem when he writes: "How
much more responsible (and guilty) can you get than, on the one hand,
to write the rarefied lyric that Stevens writes, and, on the other, to assert
that poets help people to live their lives." *Ariel and the Police,* (Madison,
1988), 214.
13. Brazeau, 21 (defense contract bond), 61 (avoidance of policy role).

14. In a better mood, Stevens contrasted his insouciant poetic "clickety-clack," unsuited to martial anthems, with the "more decorous pom-pom-pom that people expect." *Letters,* 485. ("The A B C [pom-pom-pom] of being.") Patricia Parker hears a suggestion of Hephaistos, the lame blacksmith of the gods, behind both the "cripple" of stanza 1 of "Motive" and the smithy of stanzas 4 and 5 (Parker, "Stevens and Derrida," 85). Hephaistos used his "ponderous hammer" as both a munitions maker and an artist, famously combining the functions in the shield he made for Achilles; its border displayed the basic poetic symbols of earth, sky, sea, sun, moon, and stars, while its panels portrayed life's central realities: marriages, festivals, farming, war—and a lawsuit. *Iliad,* XVIII, 468–614.
15. Cf. what Stevens said of Frost in 1954: "Frost is greatly admired by many people. I do not know his work well enough to be either impressed or unimpressed . . . His work is full (or is said to be full) of humanity." *Letters,* 825. The claim not to know Frost's poetry is at least doubtful; see Brazeau, 104. The wistful sneer "full of humanity" speaks volumes to anyone who has read Stevens's laments for his "unattainable jewel, the normal."
16. *Letters,* 617–618. His own funeral was in fact sparsely attended and dreary; Brazeau, 296–297. Part of Stevens's difference was that he was American; he noted in the same letter that the funeral in France of Paul Valéry, a poet at least as "abnormal" as Stevens, had been "a great affair." (Did he know that verses by Valéry had been chosen for inscription on a major public monument, the Chaillot Palace, in 1937?) In the same letter, Stevens also spoke of the legend that had grown up around Rilke. If we had not been reassured by T. S. Eliot that there is no competition among poets, we might almost think Stevens was reviewing the *tombeaux* of his chief competitors.
17. The interpreter, he wrote, is obliged "to base his remarks on what he has before him. It is not a question of what an author meant to say but of what he has said. In the case of a competent critic the author may well have a great deal to find out about himself and his work." *Letters,* 346. See the very strong statement to the same effect, ibid., 390; and see also 793 ("I believe in pure *explication de texte* . . . my principal form of piety").
18. "A poem is like a man walking on the banks of a river, whose shadow is reflected in the water. If you explain a poem you are likely to do it either in terms of the man or in terms of the shadow, but you have to explain it in terms of the whole. When I said recently that a poem was what was on a page, it seems to me now that I was wrong because that is explaining in terms of the man." *Letters,* 354.

19. Reality as the masculine world of money and force (war, and by extension law) works as a reading of the poem, but by no means excludes other plausible interpretations. Helen Vendler sees the forging poet as one whom maturity confronts with the imperative to weld the particulars of experience together into a firm and fixed unity, leaving behind the youthful perspectivist who, while rich in varied insights, had no solid identity or point of view. Vendler, *Words Chosen Out of Desire*, 23–26. Eleanor Cook also sees the forge as a poet's workplace, and the demand of primary noon as the writer's exhilarating yet frightening task of hammering inchoate thoughts and images into definite words. Eleanor Cook, *Poetry, Word-Play, and World-War in Wallace Stevens* (Princeton, 1988), 182–84. These readings contrast two phases of the poetic process as the referents of imagination and reality, and bring out the fear of the loss of poetic creativity that is certainly a theme in the poem—as is, of course, the fear of death, which awaits beyond autumn's changes.

20. David Walker, *The Transparent Lyric: Reading and Meaning in the Poetry of Stevens and Williams* (Princeton, 1984), 80.

21. Spring and autumn are of course themselves metaphoric vehicles for youth and late middle age—but the seasons of life form a metaphor so familiar as to pass almost unnoticed.

22. "Asides on the Oboe," *CP*, 250.

23. The shift also sustains our sense of choice: in the original time frame, fall is the present and thus there can be no going back to summer; but even in fall, we can still choose noon-reality over twilight-imagination.

24. This discussion is much indebted both to Cook, *Word-Play*, 171–188 and to Parker, "Stevens and Derrida."

25. Percy Bysshe Shelley, "A Defense of Poetry," in Harold Bloom, ed., *Selected Poetry and Prose of Shelley* (New York, 1966), 418; Stevens, "Three Academic Pieces," *NA*, 81–82.

26. Thus, Harold Bloom alludes to this poem of Stevens's while discussing Shelley's ode to his invisible skylark: "What can barely be heard, and not seen at all, is still discovered to be a basis on which to rejoice, and indeed becomes an inescapable motive for metaphor, a dark justification for celebrating the light of uncommon day." Bloom, "Introduction," *Selected Poetry and Prose of Shelley*, xxvii.

27. "Creations of Sound," *CP*, 310–311. (The poet X bears a suspicious resemblance to Stevens's old friend and rival William Carlos Williams, justly celebrated for the sharp clarity of the visual images that dominate his verse.) For Stevens's own use of sound imagery, see also "Credences of Summer," iv, *CP*, 374, one of his favorite passages from his own work: "There the distant fails the clairvoyant eye / And the secondary senses of the ear / Swarm, not with secondary sounds, but choirs . . . Pure rhetoric

of a language without words." See also the interplay of (clear) vision with (mysterious) rain-sound in "Ordinary Evening," xiii–xv, *CP,* 474–476; and the reference to the poet as "speaker / Of a speech only a little of the tongue" ("Notes," II, ix, *CP,* 397).

28. "Keep quiet in the heart, O wild bitch. O mind / Gone wild . . . Be still . . . Hear what he says, / The dauntless master, as he starts the human tale." "Puella Parvula," *CP,* 456.

29. "Man Carrying Thing," *CP,* 350–351. "It is necessary to propose an enigma to the mind. The mind always proposes a solution." "Adagia," *OP,* 168.

30. This last image, evoking Harold Bloom's figure of *apophrades* (return from the dead), seems an especially likely candidate for the "man carrying thing." Stevens's beloved *Oxford English Dictionary* tells us that the unfamiliar adjective "brune" is Old English for "burning"; it is also French for "brown," root of "brunette." Both senses evoke Dante's Brunetto of *Inferno,* xv, a dead poetic master burned brown by hellfire—"in the brown baked features / The eyes of a familiar compound ghost / Both intimate and unidentifiable," as Eliot rewrites it in "Little Gidding." (Eliot's compound Brunetto seems to have blended Mallarmé and Yeats; see Ronald Bush, *T. S. Eliot* (New York, 1984), 159, 228–237.) But of course all strong poets have dead masters, who threaten to keep them in the shade. Eleanor Cook, *Word-Play,* 185, notes the "Brunetto" connection, and adds that "brune" is also a French noun meaning "dusk" or "twilight"—making it, all in all, one of the dictionary-addicted Stevens's hardest-working words.

31. My thanks to Helen Vendler for pointing out to me that the "bright obvious" can be the returned repressed as well as a harmless (because "motionless") physical stimulus; I now read the poem as undecided between these alternatives.

32. Wordsworth, *The Prelude,* V, 598–599.

33. Philip Larkin, "Far Out," *Collected Poems,* (London, 1988), 120.

34. *CP,* 288.

35. "Stevens and Derrida," 84–86. The break between opposition and apposition might come after "primary noon," or after "The A B C of being," or even just before "The . . . X"—though the last reading leaves the forge images united with primary noon and separated from the X, and so gives up the advantage noted in the next sentence of text.

36. In further support of the secondary reading, it is worth noting that in Stevens's own only comment on "The Motive for Metaphor," he referred to it not in gloomy but rather in celebratory terms as "an illustration . . . that the essence of change is that it gives pleasure: that it exhilarates." *Letters,* 430. He often said the poet must stay open to the flux of experi-

ence and unfinished, hence never quite himself. Even in the last year of his life he wrote that "once one is strongly defined, no other definition is ever possible, in spite of daily change." *Letters,* 880. To this effect, see ibid., 289, 333, 570 (praising someone as "always a potential figure"), 680, 710 ("I have no wish to arrive at a conclusion"), 827, 839 (expressing gloom at the definitive act of collecting his poems). In "The Creations of Sound," *CP,* 310, he criticizes the rival poet, X, as "a man too exactly himself." In *Ariel and the Police,* 196—216, Frank Lentricchia seems to me to miss this exuberant aspect of Stevens's restlessness; he sees in it only ennui, ascribable to life under capitalism.

37. "Narrative always says less than it knows, but it often makes known more than it says." Gérard Genette, *Narrative Discourse: An Essay in Method* (Ithaca, 1980), 198. The interaction of narrative instability with legal judgment in *Billy Budd* is brilliantly shown in a masterwork of law-and-literature analysis, Barbara Johnson's "Melville's Fist: The Execution of *Billy Budd,*" in Johnson, *The Critical Difference* (Baltimore, 1980), 79—109.

38. Vendler, *Words Chosen Out of Desire,* 23—24.

39. The interpretations noted in the text by no means exhaust the possibilities for this gnomic phrase. I note four others:

a. Stevens may have meant to set off "steel against intimation"—which he parenthesized with dashes—against the whole series of forge images. Then it would embed a representation of the poem's overall structuring conflict between the worlds of imagination and reality, with "intimation" suggesting the obscure realm of the first three stanzas, while "steel" metonymically connotes the forge as a whole. This leaves "intimation" without a concrete referent, while "steel" designates something within the forge. Yet this asymmetry may have its point, emblematic of the poem's central crossing motif: reality is only figuratively intimated (by "steel"), whereas intimation is straightforwardly named.

b. Steven Winter suggests, in private correspondence, that "steel against intimation" is a parenthetical command, with "steel" the verb, bracing us against the intimation of mortality marked finally by the dominant, fatal, arrogant crossbones, X.

c. The referent of "intimation" might be the heat-softened iron worked by the smith's steel hammer. This keeps the imagery consistent with the surrounding lines, and puts "steel against intimation" in close apposition to its predecessor phrase, "the hard sound." Yet detracting from this reading is the inaptness of superheated metal as a correlative for "intimation."

d. Patricia Parker suggests that Stevens may be echoing Browning's *The Ring and the Book,* a poem framed by the metaphor of the poet as a goldsmith, who infuses the pure gold of fact with the alloy of imagination and then shapes (with steel) the soft metal (intimation) into an artwork, a ring. "Stevens and Derrida," 86. Browning even speaks of "the very A. B. C. of fact" (i, 708), the facts he works with are taken from the record of a legal dispute, and his philosophic-aesthetic concerns and convictions ("Is fiction which makes fact alive, fact too?" i, 705; "Art may do a thing / Obliquely, do the thing shall breed the thought," xii, 855–856) are close to Stevens's, as Parker notes. But the ruddy temper, hard sound, and sharp flash of Stevens's blacksmith are much more violent than the cool and delicate tapping and filing of Browning's goldsmith.

40. Barbara Babcock pointed out this possibility to me. Did blacksmiths traditionally use fire, hammer, and anvil to work *steel* as well as ordinary iron? Yes—at least, fancy, Hephaistos-descended, swordmaking blacksmiths did (I don't know about their horseshoeing village cousins). See Henry Wilkinson, *Engines of War* (London, 1841), 211–215; *Encyclopedia Britannica,* 22, 9th ed. (New York, 1895), s. v. "Swords." 22: 803. Steelsmithing (the heating, shaping, rapid cooling, then tempering by reheating, of carbon-hardened iron) goes back at least to Homeric Greece; see the gruesome simile describing Odysseus' blinding of the Cyclops, *Odyssey,* ix, 391–393, discussed in Wilkinson, *Engines of War,* 195–196.

V. A Change Not Quite Completed

1. James Boyd White, "The Judicial Opinion and the Poem," in White, *Heracles' Bow* (Madison, 1985), 123.

2. For the identification of Stevens as an American pragmatist, see Richard Poirier, *The Renewal of Literature,* (New York, 1987); and Frank Lentricchia, *Ariel and the Police.* (Madison, 1988).

3. See "Pragmatism," in John McDowell, ed., *The Writings of William James,* (Chicago, 1977), 364–365, 369–371, for the mediation of tough and tender.

4. The current materialist schools include law and economics and public-choice theory, while the relatively idealist approaches include much law-and-literature work, and aspects of critical legal studies, feminist jurisprudence, and critical race theory—the jurisprudential schools for which "the social construction of reality" is a central slogan.

5. In formulating this opposition, I use the literary-critical and philosophical terms "romantic" and "idealist" as equivalents, and as contrasting to the protean "realist," which does duty in both domains. A more rigorous (or minute) analysis would sort out not just two but *four* different distinctions that are here conflated. Two are literary-aesthetic: romantic vs. classic (aesthetic of the open, awe-inspiring, sublime vs. aesthetic of the closed, satisfying, beautiful); and fantasist vs. realist (openly fictive portrayal vs. mimetic portrayal). Two are philosophical: idealist vs. materialist (reality as sense-data or Platonic forms vs. reality as atoms-and-the-

void), and conceptualist vs. nominalist (general terms as having sense as well as reference vs. their having only reference). To compound the confusion, what I call "conceptualism" in this last opposition is often called "realism"; this terminology reverses the polarity and makes my idealist into a realist.

6. In legal theory, proponents of "the social construction of reality" characteristically stress both the importance and the value of metaphor in legal thought and language; conversely, positivists commonly see legal metaphors as merely decorative, distressingly vague, and potentially deceitful.

7. *OP*, 204. For other identifications of poetry with metaphor, see "Three Academic Pieces," *NA*, 81; "Effects of Analogy," *NA*, 118.

8. For Stevens's generally nonpejorative use of the term "unreal," see the already-quoted concluding couplet of "To the One of Fictive Music," *CP*, 88; see also *CP*, 313, 363, 377, 451, 468, 483, 485; *OP*, 117; *NA*, viii, 4, 150. Some critics have thought he means to denigrate the singers when "Far in the woods they sang their unreal songs / Secure," in "Credences of Summer," *CP*, 376; I think not.

9. "Noble Rider," *NA*, 36.

10. *OP*, 180; and see "A Poet That Matters," *OP*, 217–222. Robert Frost, another pragmatist Romantic, wrote of escape and quest (referring to himself, but the terms apply well to Stevens) in "Escapist—Never": "Any who seek him seek in him the seeker. / His life is a pursuit of a pursuit forever." Frost, *In the Clearing* (New York, 1962), 27.

11. "Three Academic Pieces," *NA*, 81–82.

12. *CP*, 373; for other treatments of metaphor as "evasive" see *CP*, 199, 272, 486; and see especially "Notes," I, i, *CP*, 380–381.

13. "Angel Surrounded by Paysans," *CP*, 496–497.

14. *CP*, 162; *OP* 254, 164; cf. "Blue Guitar," xxxii, *CP*, 183: "do not use the rotted names."

15. Most famously in "The Snow Man," *CP*, 9; but the ideal stayed with him to the end. See "The Plain Sense of Things," *CP*, 502, "A Clear Day and No Memories," *OP*, 138, and "On the Way to the Bus," *OP*, 136. Stevens's seasonal cycle roughly matched up with the "imagination" and "reality" cycle thus: winter (reductive realism: "The Snow Man"); spring (romantic imagination: "Notes," III, i–ii); summer (fulsome realism: "Credences of Summer"); autumn (tragic imagination: "Auroras of Autumn"). He wrote most of his poetry in spring and autumn, when the weather favored the long walks that he seemed to require for composition.

16. "Art exists that one may recover the sensation of life . . . The technique of art is to make objects 'unfamiliar.'" Victor Shklovsky, "Art as Technique," in Lee Lemon and Marion Reis, eds. and trans., *Russian Formalist Criticism* (Lincoln, Nebr., 1965), 12.

17. "Credences of Summer," *CP*, 373.

18. The irony is more evident in "Notes," I, i, *CP,* 380: "You must become an ignorant man again / And see the sun again with an ignorant eye," after which "The sun / must bear no name, gold flourisher." Stevens almost surely had in mind in this passage Descartes's account, in his Third Meditation, of the "first idea" that the senses give of the sun (the erroneous idea that it is a small bright disc). I suspect that Stevens also is echoing the episode where Dante is able to look directly at the sun, then sees Beatrice, and is transported beyond the merely human in a way that words cannot convey ("Transumanar significar *per verba* / non si poria"); *Paradiso,* I, 70–71. Cf. "To say more than human things with human voice, / That cannot be"; "Chocorua to Its Neighbor," xix, *CP,* 300. In his play with the sun as symbol of the literal, Stevens anticipates Derrida's well-known deconstruction of metaphor, Joseph Riddel shows in "The Climate of Our Poems," *Wallace Stevens Journal,* 7 (1983): 68–75.

19. It is found throughout his poetry, often most effectively in asides. It is the theme of the famous "Thirteen Ways of Looking at a Blackbird," *CP,* 92, which plays with the Imagism-Symbolism version of the reality-imagination opposition; and it is the primary subject of his three most doctrinal poems, "The Man with the Blue Guitar," "Description without Place," and "An Ordinary Evening in New Haven."

20. In this line from "Asides on the Oboe," *CP,* 251, we hear not only the eighth month, but also the poet Virgil addressing the politician Octavian, who aspired to be the divine Emperor Augustus. Stevens once used the line to illustrate "the subject matter of poetry," *Letters,* 377. In "An Ordinary Evening in New Haven," *CP,* 473, he speaks of "A verity of the most veracious men / The propounding of the four seasons and twelve months"; and in a similar spirit, he evokes latitudes and longitudes, and the zodiac, as exercises of social imagination, cognate to poetry, in "The Idea of Order at Key West," *CP,* 128.

21. *NA,* 149.

22. See especially James's metaphor of the "absolute bird," in *Writings of James,* 550–551; and compare Stevens's "The Bird with the Coppery, Keen Claws," *CP,* 82. The striking resemblance is noted in Margaret Peterson, *Wallace Stevens and the Idealist Tradition* (Ann Arbor, 1983), 97–100.

23. See, e.g., "The World Well Lost," in Rorty, *Consequences of Pragmatism,* (Madison, 1982), 3–18. Rorty claims to be walking away from philosophy (or Philosophy), but this simply puts him in company with the other "strong philosophers" of modern times.

24. "Connoisseur of Chaos," *CP,* 215. The finicky qualifier is Stevens's gesture toward the philosopher, who, as he realizes, will ask the perspectivist: "How could you possibly know, from within the mind, that the facts outrun the mind?"

25. I would say that "the substance that prevails" in Stevens is an amalgam, or a fluctuating average, of the aspiring divine, Canon Aspirin; the dry and well-hidden scientist, Professor Eucalyptus, of "An Ordinary Evening in New Haven"; and finally (as the other comic names suggest) the surviving ghost of the jester Crispin, of "The Comedian as the Letter C."
26. "Blue Guitar," xxiii, *CP*, 177.
27. All commentators note that Canon Aspirin's name shows him as a Canon *aspiring;* Milton famously describes Satan as *"aspiring / To set himself in Glory above his Peers,"* *Paradise Lost,* I, 38–39. The Canon's excessive aspirations constitute a more equivocal defect for Stevens than the sin of pride was for Milton.
28. "Adagia," *OP*, 189.
29. *Letters,* 430: "There are things with respect to which we willingly suspend disbelief; . . . if there is a will to believe . . . it seems to me that we can suspend disbelief with respect to a fiction as easily as we can suspend it with reference to anything else." Cf. "Adagia," *OP*, 188: "It is the belief and not the god that counts." Coleridge had spoken of literature as requiring the "willing suspension of disbelief," whereas William James wrote: "Faith means belief in something concerning which doubt is still theoretically possible; and as the test of belief is willingness to act, one may say that faith is the readiness to act in a cause the prosperous issue of which is not certified in advance . . . We cannot live at all without some degree of faith. Faith is synonymous with working hypothesis." "The Sentiment of Rationality," in *Writings of James,* 333–336; and see ibid., 717–735, 735–740 ("will" or "right to believe"). Eschewing James's inflammatory terminology, Gilbert Harman gives a persuasive analytical account and defense of the substance of James's teaching—the indispensable place of unjustified absolute beliefs in daily life—in his *Change of View* (Cambridge, Mass., 1986), 22–27.
30. But the death of absolutism brings with it unavoidable loss; Stevensian modernists "feel that the imagination is the *next greatest power* to faith." "The Relations between Poetry and Painting," *NA,* 171 (emphasis added).
31. "Ordinary Evening," i, ix, *CP,* 465, 471.
32. Ibid., x, *CP,* 472.
33. Ibid., *CP,* 469. And in Stevens, orderly dialogues such as that of Alpha and Omega are often interrupted by the unassimilable and dissonant voice of "life's nonsense," as when the Arabian with his "damned hoobla-hoobla-hoobla-how" disrupts the measured counterpoint of Alpha ("ever-early candor") and Omega ("late plural") in "Notes," I, iii, *CP,* 383.
34. To which we may add, from "Connoisseur of Chaos," *CP,* 215: "a law of inherent opposites / Of essential unity, is as pleasant as port"; and the

comical "Loneliness in Jersey City," *CP*, 210, with its refrain "the deer and the dachshund are one."

35. "Adagia," *OP*, 192; "Notes," III, viii, *CP*, 405; "Noble Rider," *NA*, 35.

36. "Notes," II, v, *CP*, 393. Some of the best criticism of Stevens is generated by exchange between those who prefer his transcending dialectical voice (say, Harold Bloom) and those who prefer his disintegrating dialogic voice (say, Helen Vendler.)

37. *Letters*, 798.

38. For violence and opinion, see Chapter IV above; Stevens's simultaneous attraction to Berkeleyan idealism and biological mechanism appears in *Letters*, 293–294; imagination, and then reality, as "the only genius" are in "Adagia," *OP*, 201; and compare *OP*, 272–273, with ibid., 226.

39. "Stevens's Gibberish," in Donoghue, *Reading America* (Berkeley, 1988), 174. The result of Donoghue's earlier effort to treat Stevens as a (Kantian) epistemologist appears in "Nuances on a Theme by Stevens," in Donoghue, *The Ordinary Universe* (New York, 1968), 221–240. For other commentators' protest against treating Stevens as an epistemologist, see Vendler, *Words Chosen Out of Desire*, 53; Frank Kermode, *Wallace Stevens*, (New York, 1960), 80; and especially the very thoughtful argument of Frank Doggett, *Stevens's Poetry of Thought* (Baltimore, 1966), 199–216.

40. "A Collect of Philosophy," *OP*, 275; cf. "The Irrational Element in Poetry," *OP*, 224: "I am not competent to discuss reality as a philosopher."

41. *Letters*, 293, 636. A long poem of his was "not the statement of a philosophic theory" (*Letters*, 430), and he had no interest in pursuing "the philosophy of my poems"; that would be to write "philosophy, not poetry; and it is poetry that I want to write." Ibid., 753. The poet "must not adapt his experience to that of the philosopher," whom he should rather "infuriate" than "go along with." "Adagia," *OP*, 196, 192.

42. Ibid., 710.

43. *Letters*, 861, 863–864.

44. "Montrachet-le-Jardin," *CP*, 264.

45. "My opinions generally change even while I am in the course of expressing them"; and "There is a perfect rout of characters in every man." Holly Stevens, ed., *Souvenirs and Prophecies*, (New York, 1977), 165–166. In his fine biographical essay, Richard Ellmann treats chameleonism as, along with coldness, one of the two main issues Stevens faced in his own struggle for identity. Ellmann, "How Wallace Stevens Saw Himself," in Frank Doggett and Robert Buttel, eds., *Wallace Stevens: A Celebration* (Pinceton, 1980), 160–163.

46. "A Collect of Philosophy," *OP*, 277.

47. Thus, he wrote down Graham Bell's remark that for "Cézanne integrity was the thing, and integrity never allowed him to become fixed at any

one point in his development." Milton Bates, ed., *Sur Plusieurs Beaux Sujects: Wallace Stevens' Commonplace Book* (Stanford, 1989), 53. And see Chapter 4, note 34, above.

48. Brazeau, 212–214.
49. "It is difficult for a man whose whole life is thought to continue as a poet. The reason (like the law, which is only a form of the reason) is a jealous mistress." *Letters,* 761. And see generally Chapter III, above.
50. "To an Old Philosopher in Rome," *CP,* 510–511.
51. "Is not the concept of final knowledge poetic?" *Letters,* 725.
52. "The Planet on the Table," *CP,* 532.
53. "Adagia," *OP,* 186.
54. When Santayana called William James's explorations of popular religious experience "slumming," James "chuckled to himself: 'Santayana's white marble mind.'" Gerald Myers, *William James: His Life and Thought* (New Haven, 1986), 462.
55. *NA,* 39–67. This was given as a talk at a disputatious gathering which included philosophers, a fact that no doubt explains its tone, somewhat sharper toward philosophy than was usual with Stevens; see Brazeau, 182–184.
56. Ibid., 54, 59–60. See also 65: "A poem is a particular of life thought of for so long that one's thought has become an inseparable part of it." In "Collect of Philosophy," he made the point that philosophical investigations of perception, such as Berkeley's, were of special interest to poets because "poetry is to a large extent an art of perception." *OP,* 272–273.
57. Both philosophers and poets "search / For reality," but the philosopher searches for "an interior made exterior" and the poet for "the same exterior made interior." "Ordinary Evening," xxii, *CP,* 481. This formulation is illuminated by the discussion of introspective psychology (or phenomenology) in the chapter "The Coalescence of Subject and Object," in I. A. Richards, *Coleridge on Imagination* (London, 1934), a book with which Stevens was very familiar; see Milton Bates, *Wallace Stevens: A Mythology of Self* (Berkeley, 1986), 259, note 25.
58. *OP,* 276–277 (emphasis added). Stevens adds that where philosophy is concerned with "discovering" the world, poetry focuses on "celebrating" it; ibid., 278.
59. Thus, in "Virile Poet," a theoretic statement is offered as "a statement of convenience," *NA,* 41; and a definition as "an expedient for getting on," *NA,* 54.
60. The case for the extensive direct influence of James on Stevens is argued and documented with much plausibility (by a Wintersian critic who thinks both James and Stevens too "irrationalist") in Peterson, *Stevens and the Idealist Tradition* 72–78, 91–163.

61. "Pragmatism," in *Writings of James*, 363–365: "The history of philosophy is to a great extent that of a certain clash of human temperaments. Undignified as such a treatment may seem to some of my colleagues . . ." And see ibid., 373–376.

62. "Virile Poet," *NA*, 54. Compare "Effects of Analogy," *NA*, 120: "A man's sense of the world is born with him and persists, and penetrates the ameliorations of education and experience of life." His work "is autobiographical in spite of every subterfuge." His "sense of the world dictates his subjects to him," and his sense of the world is a matter of "his mind and nerves."

63. "Notes," III, viii, *CP*, 404.

64. Stevens's contrast of our "substance . . . that prevails" and our "fluctuations" is in "Le Monocle de Mon Oncle," vi, *CP*, 15. Heidegger builds the concept of mood (*Stimmung*) centrally into his systematic phenomenology of human experience (*Dasein*); see Heidegger, *Being and Time* (New York, 1962), 172–179, 389–396. James himself strongly stresses the influence of mood on philosophical judgment in essays like "On a Certain Blindness in Human Beings" and "What Makes a Life Significant?" *Writings of James*, 629–660.

65. *Nicomachean Ethics*, 1109b, 14–23.

66. Oliver Wendell Holmes, Jr., "The Path of the Law," in Holmes, *Collected Legal Papers* (Boston, 1923), 181. For a biologistic pragmatist account of the "longing," see Peirce's famous account of inquiry as driven by "the irritation of doubt," in "The Fixation of Belief," *Collected Papers of Charles Sanders Peirce*, vol. 5 (Cambridge, Mass., 1934), nos. 374–375. On its adaptive character, see (a contemporary pragmatist masterpiece) Harman, *Change of View*, 22–27. Or read *Hamlet*.

67.   The mobile and the immobile flickering
      In the area between is and was are leaves,
      Leaves burnished in autumnal burnished trees

      And leaves in whirlings in the gutters, whirlings
      Around and away, resembling the presence of thought,
      Resembling the presences of thought, as if,

      In the end, in the whole psychology, the self,
      The town, the weather, in a casual litter,
      Together, said words of the world are the life of the world.

"An Ordinary Evening in New Haven," xii, *CP*, 474. The image of the psychic ingathering of the scattered leaves (pages, words) gives secular echo to Dante's vision of the light of paradise: "Nel suo profondo vidi che s'interna / legato con amore in un volume, / cio che per l'universo si squaderna." ("In its profundity I saw—ingathered / and bound by love

into one single volume / what in the universe seems separate, scattered.")
Paradiso, XXXIII, 85–87. Stevens's much-quoted last line appropriately overlaps this allusion with "In the beginning was the Word," and "I am the way, the truth, and the life."

68. Holmes, "Path of the Law," 181; "The Well Dressed Man with a Beard," *CP,* 247.

VI. The Colors of the Mind

1. Stevens's uncolloquial sense of "abstract" (for him *not* the opposite of concrete) appears when he says the poet must "abstract himself, and . . . withdraw with him into his abstraction the reality on which the lovers of truth insist." "Noble Rider," *NA,* 23. He apparently thinks of "abstraction" as something like the phenomenologists' "reduction" or "bracketing," the effort to get at experience just as it is. See, e.g., Edmund Husserl, "Author's Preface to the English Edition," in Husserl, *Ideas* (New York, 1962), 37–42. The "Abstract" canticle begins with the instruction to "see . . . with an ignorant eye," and ends with the instruction "not to console / Nor sanctify, but plainly to propound." It was roughly the office of the "Change" canticle to console or cure, and of the "Pleasure" canticle to (secularly) sanctify.

2. *OP,* 289. "Abstract" is a canticle of descent to bare reality; "Change" a canticle of transformation by imagination; and "Pleasure" a canticle of beatitude in a green and fluent mundo that joins earth and imagination. Stevens initially called "Notes" a *refacimento* (an Italian word meaning a renovation of a literary work); he planned, I conjecture, a more detailed correspondence to Dante's structure, but then found that if he "stuck closely to a development" he could not give his poetic moments true renovating power, and so broke free of the scheme to produce his final anarchic order of structure and fracture. See *Letters,* 431. Among the Dantean echoes that remain are the three animals of "Abstract," v (cf. *Inferno,* I), and the echoes of Dante's invocation to Apollo and subsequent sun-gazing (*Paradiso,* I) in Stevens's own invocation and in "Abstract," i. Stevens reflects more explicitly on *Paradiso,* I (interweaving Apollo-Daphne, Dante-Beatrice, and Milton's Adam-Eve) in "The Hand as a Being," *CP,* 271, apparently originally written as a canto for "Notes." (Compare the discussion in Cook, *Word-Play,* 179.)

3. The argument no doubt has some sting; Richard Posner, *Law and Literature: A Misunderstood Relationship* (Cambridge, Mass., 1988), can be seen as a book-length response, making the point that practitioners of the dismal science have souls and read good books too, but that this does not shake them from their sternly tough-minded and economistic view of the serious legal world.

4. John McDowell, ed., *The Writings of James*, (Chicago, 1977), 317–345.

5. *Letters*, 87.

6. "Lamia," *Keats: Poems* (London, 1953), 137. See the account, centered around this passage, of the Romantic poets' struggle with science and scientific philosophy in M. H. Abrams, *The Mirror and the Lamp*, (New York, 1953), 298–335. Keats's attitude toward "philosophy," in "Lamia" and elsewhere, was more complex than the quoted lines suggest.

7. *CP*, 71.

8. "Extracts from Addresses to the Academy of Fine Ideas," *CP*, 256.

9. Yvor Winters, "Wallace Stevens, or the Hedonist's Progress," in Charles Doyle, ed., *Wallace Stevens: The Critical Heritage*, (London, 1985), 227 (emphasis added.) Winters argued that Stevens, the author of "Sunday Morning," which he called "one of the greatest contemplative poems in English" and "scarcely less than Shakespearean" (ibid. 226, 239), had been ruined as a poet by a false Epicurean philosophy.

10. *Writings of James*, 364–365, 369–371. James was speaking of the rationalism of Hegel and Royce, rather than that of Descartes, Leibniz, and Spinoza; but the point holds, less obviously, for them as well.

11. *CP*, 9.

12. "A Clear Day and No Memories," *OP*, 139.

13. Giordano Bruno, as quoted by Stevens in "A Collect of Philosophy," *OP*, 267. Compare Wordsworth's famous image of Newton as a Romantic quest-hero, "Voyaging through strange seas of Thought, alone." Wordsworth, *The Prelude*, iii, 63–64. Stevens also well understood Pascal's opposite (and among modern poets more influential) reaction to Copernicus, terror at the silence of the empty spaces: "How cold the vacancy / When the phantoms are gone and the shaken realist / First sees reality." "Esthétique du Mal," viii, *CP*, 320.

14. *CP*, 125–126; see *Letters*, 293, for Stevens's own fondness for this poem, which I do not share.

15. "On the Way to the Bus," *OP*, 136.

16. Christopher Columbus Langdell, *Cases on Contracts* (Boston, 1871), viii–ix.

17. *CP*, 424.

18. *CP*, 375. Stevens was a Holmes reader; see Milton Bates, ed., *Sur Plusieurs Beaux Sujects: Wallace Stevens' Commonplace Book* (Stanford, 1989), 75.

19. "The Idea of Order at Key West," *CP*, 128–130.

20. In "Things of August," ix, *CP*, 494–495, Stevens imagines a kind of poet's positive law, a modern, collectively self-legislated, existentialist supreme fiction, a "scribble of fret and fear and fate . . . free from question, / Because we wanted it so . . . A text of intelligent men / At the center of the unintelligible."

21. "To an Old Philosopher in Rome," *CP,* 510–511.
22. "Notes," I, iii, *CP,* 382.
23. "The Path of the Law," 181.
24. Ibid., 122–123. Frank Lentricchia takes the title of his recent book on William James, Foucault, and Stevens from this passage.
25. "Notes," I, iii, *CP,* 383. Very good on this subject is Irving Ehrenpreis, "Strange Relation: Stevens's Nonsense," in Frank Doggett and Robert Buttel, eds., *Wallace Stevens: A Celebration* (Princeton, 1980), 219–234.
26. "The Planet on the Table," *CP,* 532.
27. "On the Road Home," *CP,* 203–204.
28. "Landscape with Boat," *CP,* 241. Recall Stevens's byplay with "primary" and "secondary" in "Man Carrying Thing," discussed in Chapter IV.
29. "Esthétique du Mal," xv, *CP,* 325.
30. "Sunday Morning," vi, 69.
31. "This Solitude of Cataracts," *CP,* 425; "Ordinary Evening," x, *CP,* 472.
32. *CP,* 64.
33. *Inferno,* XXXIV, 28–29.
34. *CP,* 426. The "purple muse" recalls Hoon, of "Tea at the Palaz of Hoon" (*CP,* 65), who "in purple . . . descended / The western day through what you called / The loneliest air." Hoon in turn recalls Wordsworth's much-debated "presence" (real or imagined?), "Whose dwelling is the light of setting suns, / And the round ocean and the living air, / And the blue sky, and in the mind of man" ("Tintern Abbey," 97–99). Stevens accepts the "presence" as fictive, a predecessor to the angel of "Notes," III, viii.
35. Richard Weisberg, *The Failure of the Word: The Protagonist as Lawyer in Modern Fiction* (New Haven, Conn., 1984).
36. Cf. Harold Bloom: "The great enemy of poetry in the Romantic tradition has never been reason, but rather those premature modes of conceptualization that masquerade as final accounts of reason in every age." Bloom, *The Ringers in the Tower,* (Chicago, 1971), 323.

Conclusion

1. I pursue this project in a long article, soon forthcoming in expanded form as a book; see "Introduction," note 11.
2. "To speak of joy and sing of it, borne on / The shoulders of joyous men . . . / This is a facile exercise." "Notes," III, i, *CP,* 398. By contrast, he said that the "thing I like more than anything else" in the reception of a poem was a reader's report that "it gave him pleasure." *Letters,* 429.
3. Vendler, "The Hunting of Wallace Stevens," in Vendler, *The Music of What Happens* (Cambridge, Mass., 1988), 75–76.
4. "Montrachet-le-Jardin," *CP,* 260. I still don't know what a "chidder-

barn" is; I think of the blue bulls as a reminiscence of a crèche (with kneeling oxen) remembered from childhood, as in Hardy's "The Oxen."

5. "Natural Law," in Holmes, *Collected Legal Papers,* (Boston, 1923), 314–315, 316.
6. *CP,* 263.
7. See, for instance, Stanley Fish, "Consequences," in Fish, *Doing What Comes Naturally* (Durham, N.C., 1989), 315–342. Fish argues from an algorithmic conception of theory that seems inappropriate outside the exact sciences. "Theory," as I use the term (and I think I follow usage), is simply whatever discourse is potentially applicable to practice, and yet thought by the average practitioner too general or too abstracted from reality to be useful.
8. "Pragmatism," in John McDowell, ed., *The Writings of William James,* (Chicago, 1977), 368.
9. Revelation 3:15–16. Cf. Fish, "Why No One's Afraid of Wolfgang Iser," *Doing What Comes Naturally,* 68–86.
10. "Coleridge," in Mill, *Utilitarianism and Other Essays* (London, 1987), 181.
11. Bertrand Russell, *A History of Western Philosophy* (New York, 1945), 172–173. Robin West turns this passage against Judge Posner in her review of his *Law and Literature;* see West, "Law, Literature, and the Celebration of Authority," *Northwestern Law Review,* 83 (1989), 1008–1009.
12. *Writings of James,* 375.
13. Stevens is throughout a riddler, which may explain part of his appeal for lawyers; see on this aspect of his poetry, Eleanor Cook, "Riddles, Charms, and Fictions," in Harold Bloom, ed., *Wallace Stevens* (New York, 1985), 151–164.
14. *CP,* 215–216; for the allusive reverberations of the image, see M. H. Abrams, *Natural Supernaturalism,* (New York, 1975), 448–462.
15. "Notes," III, i, *CP,* 399.
16. Kenneth Burke, *Counter-Statement,* 2nd ed. (Berkeley, 1953), 90.
17. "Prologues to What Is Possible," *CP,* 516.

Credits

An expanded version of Chapter 4 appeared in the *Yale Journal of Law and the Humanities*, and is reprinted with permission.

Most of Chapter 5 and portions of the Conclusion appeared in the *Southern California Law Review*, and are reprinted with permission. The author would also like to thank the respective publishers for permission to reproduce the following:

Excerpts from *The Collected Poems of Wallace Stevens, Opus Posthumous,* and *The Necessary Angel,* by Wallace Stevens, and from *Letters of Wallace Stevens,* edited by Holly Stevens. Reprinted by permission of Alfred A. Knopf Inc.

Excerpts from *Selected Poems of Wallace Stevens* and *The Collected Poems of Wallace Stevens,* by Wallace Stevens. Reprinted by permission of Faber and Faber Ltd.

Excerpt from "So Long? Stevens" from *The Dream Songs,* by John Berryman. Copyright © 1959, 1962, 1963, 1964, 1965, 1966, 1967, 1968, 1969 by John Berryman. Reprinted by permission of Farrar, Straus and Giroux, Inc.

Excerpts from "Aubade," "Far Out," and "Toads Revisited" from *Collected Poems,* by Philip Larkin. Copyright © 1988, 1989 by the Estate of Philip Larkin. Reprinted by permission of Farrar, Straus and Giroux, Inc.

Excerpt from *Mirabell: Books of Number,* by James Merrill. Reprinted by permission of James Merrill.

Excerpts from "Page from the Koran," from *Late Settings,* by James Merrill. Copyright © 1985 by James Merrill. Reprinted by permission of Macmillan Publishing Company.

Excerpts from *The Divine Comedy of Dante Alighieri,* translated by Allen Mandelbaum, copyright © 1982 by Allen Mandelbaum, on the English translation. Used by permission of Bantam books, a division of Bantam, Doubleday, Dell Publishing Group, Inc.

Excerpts from Paul Valéry, "Le Cimetière Marin," translated by David Paul, from *Paul Valéry: An Anthology,* edited by James Lawler, used by permission of Princeton University Press.

Index

"Adagia," 19, 22, 31, 52, 76, 78, 82
"American Change" (Ginsberg), 120n55
"Anecdote of the Prince of Peacocks,"
130n39
"Angel Surrounded by Paysans," 70
Aristotle, 85, 87, 107
Arnold, Matthew, 15
"Arrival at the Waldorf," 27
Art as Experience (Dewey), 31
"Asides on the Oboe," 60, 72
"As You Leave the Room," 133n6
Auden, W. H., 2, 7, 118n16
"Auroras of Autumn, The," 28
"Axel" (Villiers de l'Isle-Adam), 33

Babcock, Barbara, 138n40
Bacon, Francis, 80
Bates, Milton, 14
Bell, Graham, 142n47
Benjamin, Walter, 33, 34
Bentham, Jeremy, 32, 73, 74, 89
Berryman, John, 12
Billy Budd (Melville), 9
Blake, William, 73, 74
Bloom, Harold, 26, 135n26, 136n30,
147n36
Booth, Wayne, 123n26
Brazeau, Peter, 13, 15
Brinnin, John Malcolm, 13
Browning, Robert, 137n39
Bryant, William Cullen, 119n29
Burdge, Clifford, 43
Burke, Kenneth, 110

Caillois, Roger, 41, 43, 81
Canoe Club, 50
Cassirer, Ernst, 72
Catholicism, 124n29
Church, Henry, 47

"Clear Day and No Memories, A," 93
Coleridge, Samuel Taylor, 32, 37,
141n29
Collected Poems, 29
"Collect of Philosophy," 81, 83
"Comedian as the Letter C, The,"
123n21
"Connoisseur of Chaos," 108–109,
140n24, 141n34
Contingency, Irony, and Solidarity (Rorty),
31
Cook, Eleanor, 135n19, 136n30
Corn, Naaman, 23
Cover, Robert, 23
"Creations of Sound, The," 61, 136n36
"Credences of Summer," 52, 71, 94,
135n27
Critical Legal Studies movement, 38,
138n4
Critical response to Stevens, 12–14

Dante Alighieri, 100, 136n30, 140n18,
144n67, 145n2
"Death of a Soldier," 30
"Deceptions" (Larkin), 123n25
"Defense of Poetry, A" (Shelley), 123n26
Derrida, Jacques, 140n18
Descartes, René, 81, 88, 91, 140n18,
146n9
"Description without Place," 40
Dewey, John, 31
Divine Comedy (Dante), 86, 130n46
Doggett, Frank, 13
Donne, John, 2
Donoghue, Denis, 79
Dworkin, Ronald, 3

Ecclesiastes, 80
Education, legal, 2, 7, 52

151

Index

ration, 3–4, 9, 67; historical tradition behind, 14–15; Stevens and, 14,
26–27, 103; linguistic version of,
22–23, 27, 35, 36, 38, 39–40, 41;
psychological version of, 22–23, 31;
humanist themes, 23, 58, 89; legal
theory and, 41, 68; scholarship, 53,
68
Leibniz, Gottfried, 91, 146n9
Lentricchia, Frank, 13, 124n35,
133n12, 136n36, 147n24
Locke, John, 36–37, 38, 39, 40, 41,
48, 50, 81, 98; theory of language,
65, 66, 88
"Loneliness in Jersey City," 141n34
Lorde, Andre, 7
"Lot of People Bathing in a Stream, A,"
56

Mallarmé, Stéphane, 30
"Man Carrying Thing," 62
"Man with the Blue Guitar, The," 40–
41, 75, 140n19
Materialist schools, 138n4
McCarthy, Mary, 13
"Men Made Out of Words," 14, 40
Metaphor, 37, 40, 41, 43, 110–111;
vs. reality, 53, 55, 61, 62, 63, 69,
70, 71; obscurity and, 54, 59, 61–
62, 64, 73; law and, 58, 65; poetry
and, 70
Mill, John Stuart, 32, 107
Milosz, Czeslaw, 7
Milton, John, 19, 141n27
"Monocle de Mon Oncle, Le," 144n64
Montaigne, Michel, 80
"Montrachet-le-Jardin," 80, 104
Moore, Marianne, 12, 19
Morris, William, 30
"Motive for Metaphor, The," 8, 53–56,
57, 58–61, 63–64, 65, 66–67, 80–
81
Mullen, Ralph, 122n15

Narrative, 26–27, 37, 66
"Natural Law" (Holmes), 105

Neruda, Pablo, 7
Newton, Isaac, 88, 90, 91
Nietzsche, Friedrich Wilhelm, 30, 32,
65, 66, 72, 76, 80, 93
"Noble Rider," 31, 56, 145n1
"No Possum, No Sop, No Taters," 20
"Notes toward a Supreme Fiction," 20,
28, 75–76, 78, 84, 96, 97, 140n18;
organization of, 86

O'Dowd, Charles, 42–43, 122n15,
129n24
"Of Mere Being," 5
"Of Modern Poetry," 27
"On the Road Home," 98
Opus Posthumous, 19
"Ordinary Evening in New Haven, An,"
40, 68, 77, 86, 140nn19,20,
143n56, 144n67
Owen, Wilfred, 57
"Owl's Clover," 29, 33, 125n41

"Palme" (Valéry), 116n15
Papini, Giovanni, 33
Paradise Lost (Milton), 19, 22, 141n27
Paradiso (Dante), 144n67, 145n2
Parker, Patricia, 64, 132n3, 134n14,
137n39
Pascal, Blaise, 50, 51, 80, 146n13
Pater, Walter, 30
Perspectivism, 69–70, 72–73, 74–75,
76, 77, 79, 86
Philosophy and poetry, 79–85, 105–111
"Phoenix and the Turtle, The" (Shake-
speare), 116n15
"Planet on the Table, The," 82, 98
Plato, 35, 36, 98
Pleasure, 86–88, 90, 91–92, 95, 96–
97
"Poems of Our Climate, The," 100
"Poetry Is a Destructive Force," 33
"Poet That Matters, A," 4
Politics: Stevens and, 29–34
Positivism, 41, 64, 69, 128n18
Posner, Richard, 1–2, 50n, 52, 59, 69,
145n3